Easy PowerPoint® for Windows® 95

Elizabeth Eisner Reding

Easy PowerPoint for Windows 95

Copyright © 1995 by Que® Corporation.

Library of Congress Catalog Card Number: 95-71423

International Standard Book Number: 0-7897-0627-X

98 97 96 95   8 7 6 5 4 3 2 1

Interpretation of the printing code: the rightmost double-digit number is the year of the book's first printing; the rightmost single-digit number is the number of the book's printing. For example, a printing code of 95-1 shows that this copy of the book was printed during the first printing of the book in 1995.

Screen reproductions in this book were created by means of the program Collage Plus from Inner Media, Inc., Hollis, NH.

This book was produced digitally by Macmillan Computer Publishing and manufactured using 100% computer-to-plate technology (filmless process), by Shepard Poorman Communications Corporation, Indianapolis, Indiana.

Credits

Publisher
Roland Elgey

Vice President and Publisher
Marie Butler-Knight

Publishing Manager
Barry Pruett

Editorial Services Director
Elizabeth Keaffaber

Managing Editor
Michael Cunningham

Acquisitions Coordinator
Martha O'Sullivan

Product Development Specialist
Lori Cates

Production Editor
Audra Gable

Copy Editor
Rebecca Mayfield

Technical Editor
Marty Wyatt

Book Designers
Barbara Kordesh
Amy Peppler-Adams

Cover Designers
Dan Armstrong
Kim Scott

Production Team
Claudia Bell, Jason Carr, Anne
Dickerson, Mike Henry, Damon Jordan,
Daryl Kessler, Scott Tullis

Indexer
Carol Sheehan

Composed in *Stone Serif* and *MCPdigital* by Que Corporation

About the Author

Although a native of the east coast, **Liz Reding** now lives in the beautiful splendor of northwest New Mexico. She writes computer books, consults and trains individuals and corporated clients, and teaches at the Gallup branch of the University of New Mexico. To date, Liz has written computer books on Microsoft Excel, Microsoft PowerPoint, Novell Quattro Pro, Freelance Graphics, and Lotus 1-2-3. She has provided technical edits for Que on many other subjects, including such Internet topics as Netscape and HTML.

In her copious spare time, she rides her mountain bike, renovates her house, and makes sure her cats have enough to eat.

Trademark Acknowledgments

Contents

Easy PowerPoint for Windows 95

Part VII: Working in Outline View — 163

Part VIII: Creating Notes and Handouts — 177

Part IX: Showing a Presentation — 193

Part X: Sample Slides — 217

Quick Reference — 230

Glossary — 237

Index — 243

Introduction

What You Can Do with PowerPoint

Microsoft PowerPoint is a fun and easy-to-use presentation graphics program. You use a presentation graphics program to create informative displays that can highlight new corporate products or services, or update others on progress toward a common goal. A PowerPoint presentation can contain charts, artwork, tables, and organizational charts, as well as special effects and sounds.

Instead of displaying your work on pages (as a word processor does), PowerPoint displays your work on the screen as *slides*. You can view one or many slides on your monitor at the same time. And when you finish your presentation, you can display it on a standard-size computer monitor or a large projection monitor, or you can print it out in a variety of ways.

PowerPoint provides all the tools you need to create a beautiful presentation with a minimum of effort: professionally designed backgrounds, preformatted page layouts, and wizards that guide you step by step through different processes. The following list gives you an overview of the things you can do with the powerful PowerPoint features.

- *Use toolbar buttons to perform common tasks.* Although you can still use menu commands, most of the tasks you perform often are just a mouse click away! The Standard and Formatting toolbars are always visible and contain buttons for the most common commands.

- *Choose a beautiful background using design templates.* Create a presentation with creative, attractive background designs that look like the work of a professional graphic artist. Each background (or design template) contains colors, patterns, and a design scheme that give your presentation continuity as well as a professional look.

- *Use different types of page layouts.* As you're creating your presentation, you may find that you want different types of information on your slides. PowerPoint contains a variety of AutoLayouts—slides that already contain a title, graphics, charts, bulleted lists, or any combination of these.

■ *Enter text easily*. You can add text to a slide easily by clicking the "Click to add text" box that contains preformatted text styles. When you click this box, a text box appears. You enter your text in the box, and you can edit, delete, or add to the text at any time.

■ *Change bullet symbols*. You can enter text on a slide as a bulleted list in which a symbol precedes each line of text. (You can even change the symbol if you want.)

■ *Format type and paragraphs*. PowerPoint provides preformatted styles that look professional and attractive. In addition, you can change the typefaces, type size, alignment, and other type attributes to enhance and personalize your presentation.

■ *Check your spelling*. Make sure you spelled the words in your presentation correctly using the spell checking utility. PowerPoint even enables you to add your own words to the dictionary.

■ *Create an organizational chart*. An organizational chart—or org chart, for short—is a great addition to any slide. You can add, delete, and move people within the chart, as well as change the style of people within groups.

■ *Add a table to your presentation*. Using PowerPoint's Insert a Microsoft Word Table button, you can take advantage of Word's incredible table capabilities. You can create a table that has multiple columns and rows, and you can format the table using the Table AutoFormat feature.

■ *Illustrate your data using a chart*. You can add a chart to your presentation using the Microsoft Graph program. You open this program, which contains a wide variety of chart styles, from within PowerPoint.

■ *Use WordArt to make your text stand out*. The WordArt feature enables you to apply special effects to text—such as making words look wavy or stretched. In addition, you can change colors and add shadow effects to your WordArt.

■ *Create Speaker's Notes, Meeting Minutes, and Action Items*. PowerPoint's Meeting Minder feature enables you to create Speaker's Notes, which you can use during your presentation to remind yourself of things you want to mention. Meeting Minutes are the slide-by-slide comments you make on the presentation. Action Items are points that you need to give attention to later.

■ *Print your presentation*. You can print your presentation in a variety of ways. You can print slides on a color or black and white printer with one slide per page or with many miniature slide images on a single page. You can even print each slide on a transparency if you want to use your presentation on an overhead projector.

■ *Create a slide show to display on a computer*. You can show your slides on a computer for others to see. When you do, you can apply special effects such as sounds, text builds, and transition effects to give your presentation a professional quality.

About the Program

This book covers Microsoft PowerPoint version 7.0 for Windows 95. With this book, you'll learn how to start the PowerPoint program from the Windows 95 Start menu, as well as from the Microsoft Office 95 toolbar. (The Office 95 suite includes Word for Windows 7.0, Excel 7.0, and PowerPoint 7.0. However, you do not have to install the Office 95 suite of programs on your computer.)

Some of the tasks within this book only work if you do have Office 95 (or its individual programs) installed. For example, Tasks 37 through 43 teach you how to create and manage a Word table within PowerPoint. You cannot perform these tasks unless Word for Windows 7.0 is installed on your computer.

In addition, some tasks in the book require that you perform a Custom installation of your software to install the special features (such as the organizational chart, clip art, and WordArt) that you need to perform the tasks. If certain features in this book don't work, try reinstalling the software and clicking the **Custom** button to see a list of the advanced features that you can install.

Task Sections

Each Task section includes the steps for accomplishing a certain task (such as adding a new slide or checking spelling). The numbered steps walk you through a specific example so that you can learn the task by actually doing it.

Big Screen

At the beginning of each task is a large picture of your PC screen showing the results of the task or some other key element from the task (such as a menu or dialog box).

"Why would I do this?"

Each task includes a brief explanation of why you would benefit from knowing how to accomplish the task.

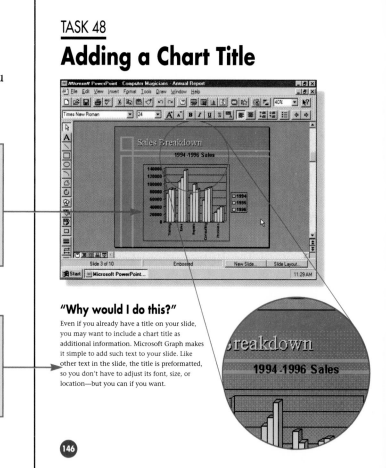

TASK 48
Adding a Chart Title

"Why would I do this?"

Even if you already have a title on your slide, you may want to include a chart title as additional information. Microsoft Graph makes it simple to add such text to your slide. Like other text in the slide, the title is preformatted, so you don't have to adjust its font, size, or location—but you can if you want.

146

Step-by-Step Screen

Each task includes a screen shot for each step of the procedure. The screen shot shows how the computer screen looks at each step in the process.

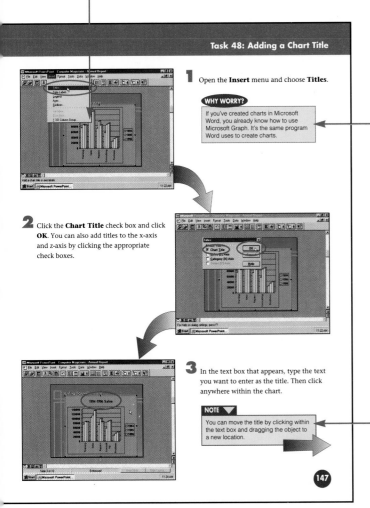

Task 48: Adding a Chart Title

1 Open the **Insert** menu and choose **Titles**.

WHY WORRY?

If you've created charts in Microsoft Word, you already know how to use Microsoft Graph. It's the same program Word uses to create charts.

2 Click the **Chart Title** check box and click **OK**. You can also add titles to the x-axis and z-axis by clicking the appropriate check boxes.

3 In the text box that appears, type the text you want to enter as the title. Then click anywhere within the chart.

NOTE

You can move the title by clicking within the text box and dragging the object to a new location.

147

Why Worry? Notes

The Why Worry? notes tell you how to undo certain procedures or how to get out of unexpected situations.

Other Notes

Many tasks include short notes that tell you a little more about the procedure. For example, these notes may define terms, explain other options, refer you to other sections, or provide hints and shortcuts.

PART I

Getting Started Quickly

Microsoft PowerPoint enables you to create beautiful, professional-
looking presentations in a matter of minutes. A *presentation* consists
of one or more *slides* that contain brief statements you can
elaborate on when you talk in front of an audience. There are lots of ways to
get your message across to viewers, but a combination of a few words and large
pictures usually works best. With PowerPoint, you can add lots of visual effects
(such as shading and color) to your slides. In addition, you can display the
data in your PowerPoint slides in a variety of ways using bulleted lists, tables,
charts, and artwork.

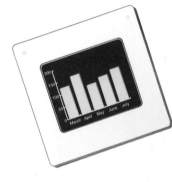

Of course, PowerPoint can only work if you have it installed on your
computer. This book covers PowerPoint for Windows 95, version 7.0. When
you install PowerPoint and open it for the first time, you see an opening
screen that explains what's new in Microsoft PowerPoint. This "guided tour"
gives you information on new features in the program. It's a great
introduction to PowerPoint's uses, tools, and features. (You can close this
tour by clicking the Minimize button in the upper-right corner of the
window.)

How you start PowerPoint depends upon whether you bought the program by
itself or as part of the Microsoft Office suite of programs. Task 1 explains both
ways of starting the program.

PowerPoint comes with all the tools you need to make your presentation look
great—including artwork. You accomplish most tasks you need to perform in
PowerPoint by clicking a button on a toolbar. Although there are lots of
buttons and toolbars, you never have to worry about forgetting which button
does what because each button has a ToolTip that tells you what it does (when
you position your mouse pointer over a toolbar button, the button's name
appears next to it). PowerPoint also includes powerful helpers called *wizards*

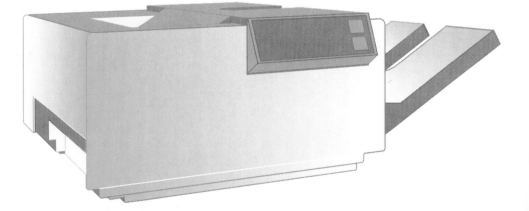

that guide you through the steps of creating your presentation. All you have to do is answer a few simple questions, and the AutoContent Wizard creates slides that contain text based on your presentation topic! Of course, you can always modify the text if you choose.

But it's not enough for your words to sound great; your presentation has to look great, too. To make your slides look terrific, PowerPoint comes with 55 design templates. (If you've used other versions of PowerPoint, you'll find that most of your favorite design templates are still available. PowerPoint's developers added a few templates and deleted a few.) These design templates not only contain professionally created colors and patterns, but also contain instructions for each slide's *layout.* The layout of each slide determines where you place text and how text looks on the slide. When you add a new slide, PowerPoint's AutoLayout feature enables you to choose the type of slide you want to add to your presentation.

Most of us don't start and complete a project in one sitting. I always put in an hour here and there whenever I have time. In order to work on your presentation when you want to and make modifications later on, you need to save the presentation on your computer. If you save your work, you can come back to your presentation and work on it again when your schedule permits. Saving your work also means you can take your presentation to another computer either to make additional changes or to show your slides at another location. You can display your presentation on a computer monitor, or if you choose, you can print out your presentation in a variety of ways. PowerPoint enables you to print slides one per page or up to six per page.

In this part of the book, you learn how to create a professional-looking presentation using PowerPoint's AutoContent Wizard. Once the presentation is complete, you add a new slide, apply a different design template, and save and print your slides. You also learn how to properly close PowerPoint and exit Windows 95.

> **NOTE** ▼
>
> When you first open PowerPoint, you may see an extra toolbar called the WorkGroup toolbar. This toolbar includes buttons that enable you to perform tasks in a networked environment. The screen pictures in this book do not show the WorkGroup toolbar. To remove this toolbar, click on View in the Main Menu bar. Then click on Toolbars. In the Toolbars dialog box, click on the WorkGroup check box to remove the check. Click OK, and the toolbar disappears.

Starting Microsoft PowerPoint

"Why would I do this?"

In order to use the features in Microsoft PowerPoint, you first have to turn on your computer and start the program. Once you start PowerPoint, you can open an existing presentation or create a brand new one.

How you start the program depends on whether you bought the program by itself or as part of the Microsoft Office suite of programs. Follow steps 1–3 if you bought PowerPoint separately; follow steps 4–6 if you got it in the Microsoft Office package.

10

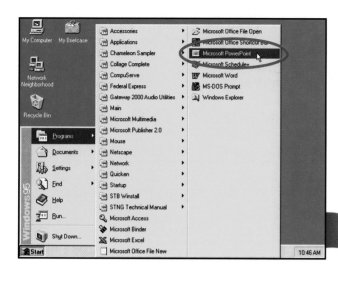

1 Click the **Start** button on the Windows 95 taskbar. The Start menu appears. You open programs and existing documents from the Start menu, and you also use the Start menu to shut down your computer before you turn it off. Using your mouse, point to **Programs**, and then click on **Microsoft PowerPoint**.

WHY WORRY?

If you mistakenly click on the wrong program, close that program and perform step 1 again.

2 If you see the Tip of the Day dialog box, click **OK** when you finish reading it. If you want to read more tips before closing this dialog box, click the **More Tips** button. If you don't want this dialog box to open when you start PowerPoint, click the **Show Tips at Startup** check box so the check mark disappears, and you won't see the dialog box again!

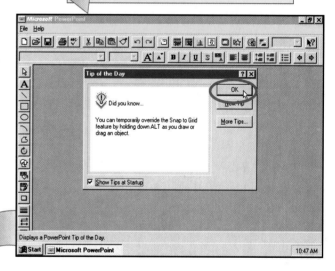

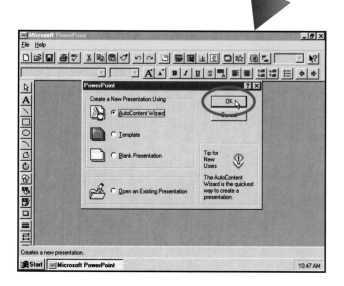

3 The PowerPoint dialog box that appears on-screen next enables you to open an existing presentation or start a new one. Make a selection and click **OK**.

4 If the Microsoft Office Shortcut Bar appears on your desktop (which it will if you have the Microsoft Office suite of programs installed on your computer), you can use it to open PowerPoint. Click the **Start a New Document** button.

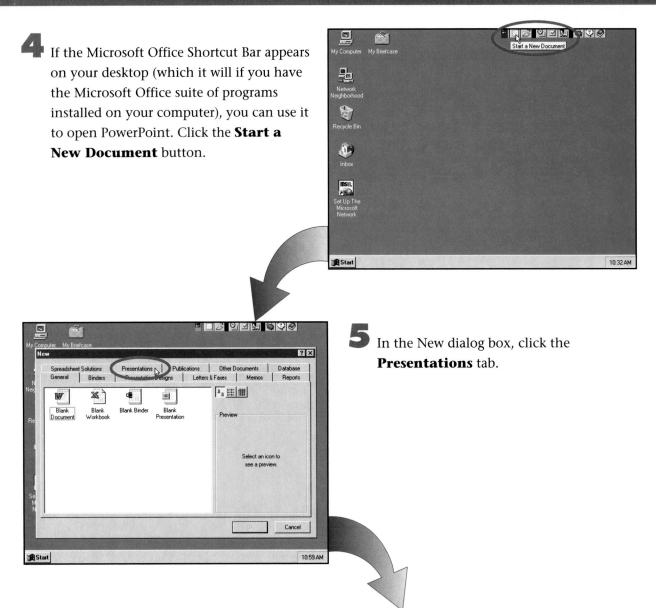

5 In the New dialog box, click the **Presentations** tab.

6 Click the **AutoContent Wizard** icon and click **OK**. PowerPoint opens and displays the AutoContent Wizard, which you'll learn how to use in the next task. ∎

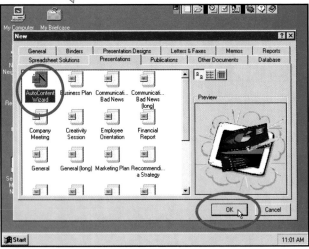

NOTE ▼

When you work in a word processing program, you create a document that contains pages with large amounts of text. When you work in a presentation graphics program such as Microsoft PowerPoint, you create a *presentation* that contains information on *slides*.

Creating a Presentation Using the AutoContent Wizard

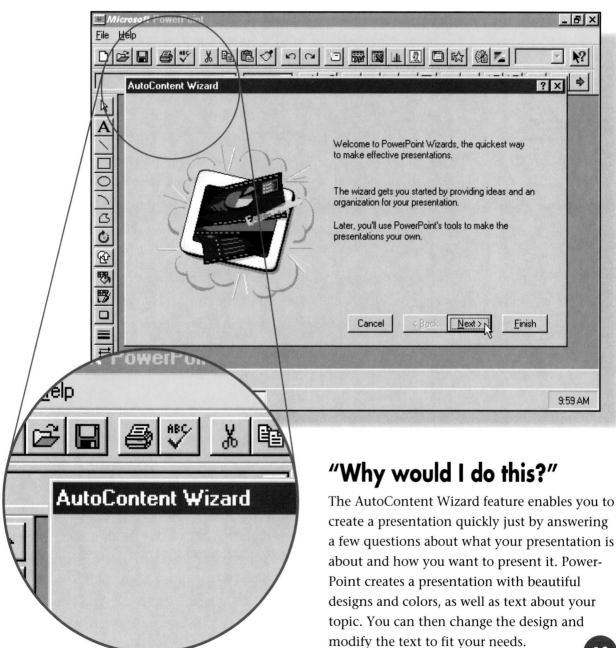

"Why would I do this?"

The AutoContent Wizard feature enables you to create a presentation quickly just by answering a few questions about what your presentation is about and how you want to present it. Power-Point creates a presentation with beautiful designs and colors, as well as text about your topic. You can then change the design and modify the text to fit your needs.

1 In the PowerPoint dialog box, the AutoContent Wizard is the default selection. (A selected option button contains a dot in the circle next to the option.) Click **OK**.

> **NOTE** ▼
>
> A dialog box option that is already selected is called the *default* selection.

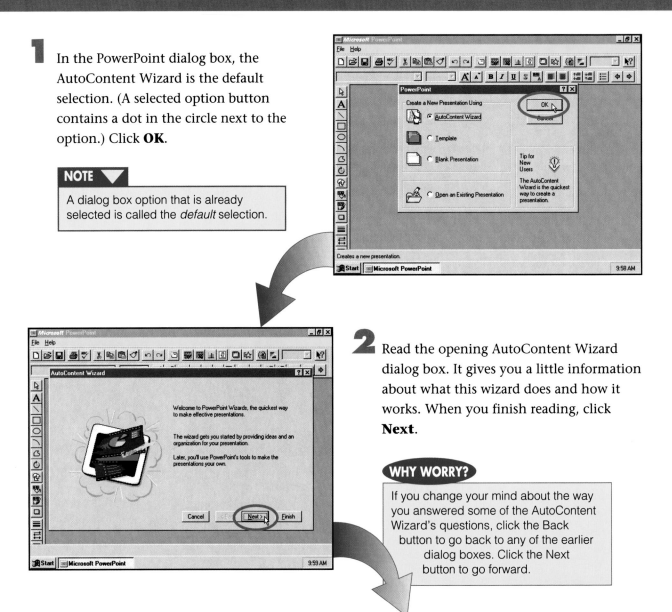

2 Read the opening AutoContent Wizard dialog box. It gives you a little information about what this wizard does and how it works. When you finish reading, click **Next**.

> **WHY WORRY?**
>
> If you change your mind about the way you answered some of the AutoContent Wizard's questions, click the Back button to go back to any of the earlier dialog boxes. Click the Next button to go forward.

3 You enter information about you, your company, and your presentation topic by clicking on each text box in the Auto-Content Wizard dialog box and then typing your information. Entering this information is optional, but what you enter here appears on the first slide in your presentation—the title slide. When you finish entering the information, click **Next**.

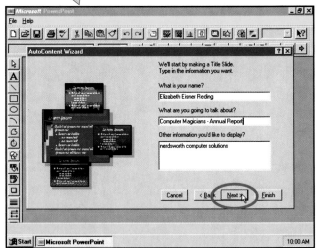

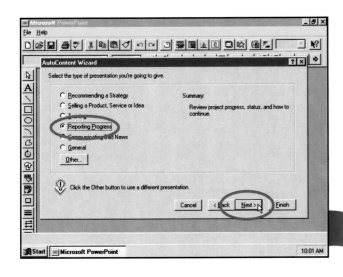

4 Click the button for the topic that best describes the theme of your presentation, and a brief description of that topic appears on the right side of the dialog box. When you're sure of the selection you've made, click **Next**.

NOTE ▼

Neither the appearance nor the content of the completed presentation is permanent; you can always change things later on.

5 Select a visual style and an approximate length for your presentation. If you're unsure about either of these options, just accept the answer that's already in the dialog box. The visual style button affects the appearance of your slides; the length affects how many slides the AutoContent Wizard includes in your presentation. When you're satisfied with your selections, click **Next**.

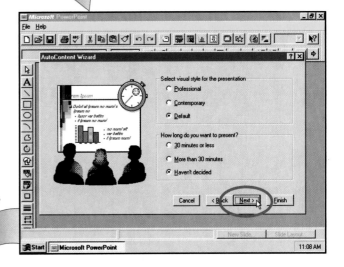

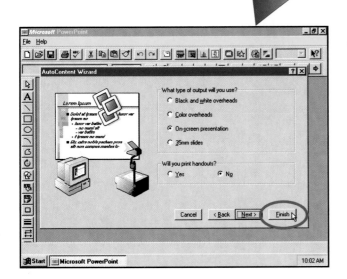

6 Click the button for the type of output you need for your presentation and indicate whether or not you want to print handouts. Click **Finish**, and PowerPoint creates a presentation based on your responses. (If you click **Next**, PowerPoint tells you your presentation is almost finished. When you see this message, click **Finish**.) When PowerPoint finishes creating the presentation, you see its title slide on-screen. ■

Looking at Slide Views

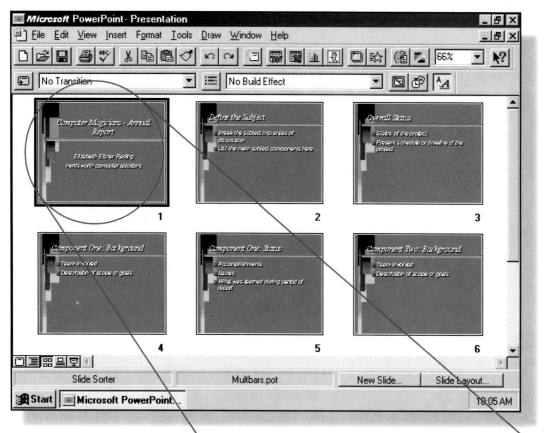

"Why would I do this?"

Sometimes you need to look at what you're working on in a different way. Have you ever backed away from a painting so you could see it better? You may need to do the same when you work on a presentation. Luckily, PowerPoint has several views that enable you to see your slides using the right amount of detail. There might be times when you need to enlarge a slide to see detail, and there might be times when you need to shrink a slide to see the whole slide.

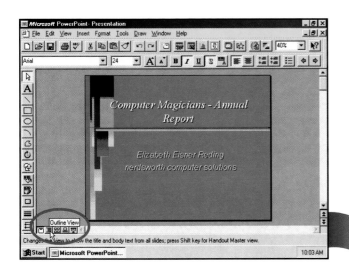

1 The slide view buttons in the lower-left corner of the screen enable you to change from one view to another. The button for the view you are currently in looks pushed in. The default view is Slide View, in which PowerPoint displays one slide at a time and you can easily read all the detail on the slide. Click the **Outline View** button to change to Outline View.

WHY WORRY?

If you accidentally click the wrong view button, just click the button for the view you really want.

2 Outline View displays the text on each slide without the artwork. The slide symbol to the left of each slide indicates if it contains graphics. None of the slides pictured here have artwork, so the slide symbols are all blank; a small picture appears on the slide symbol if there is any artwork on the slide. Click the **Notes Pages View** button to change to that view.

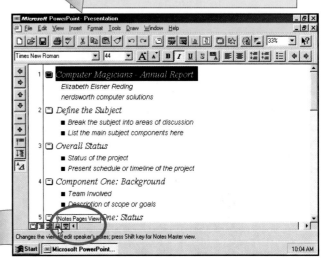

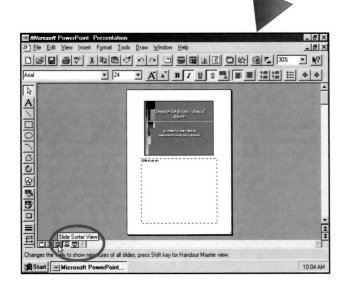

3 Notes Pages View displays a miniature version of one slide per page with space for notes. Here you can add reminders about what you want to talk about when you display the slide. Click the **Slide Sorter View** button to see all the slides in your presentation again. ■

NOTE ▼

A miniature version of a slide or graphic image is called a *thumbnail*.

Applying a Different Design Template

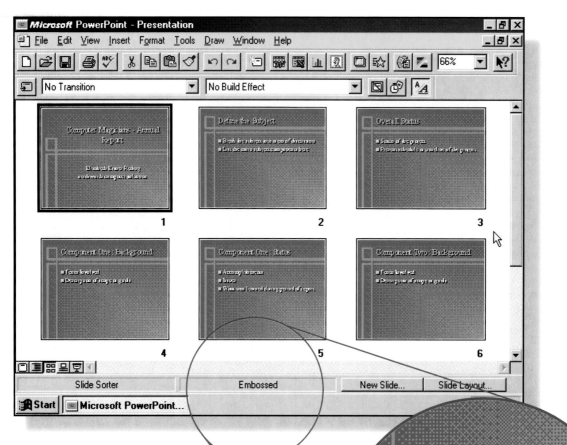

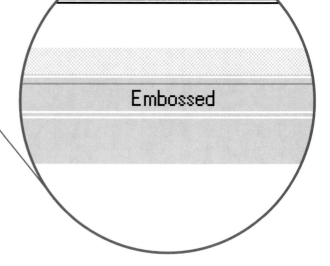

Embossed

"Why would I do this?"

When you create your presentation, PowerPoint attempts to make your slides look attractive by applying a design template that includes preset patterns and colors. PowerPoint comes with 27 design templates, and you can apply a different one anytime you want. You might, for example, want to use a different template that has brighter colors or a different design. Or you just might want to try a new and exciting color scheme!

1 From Slide Sorter view, click the **Apply Design Template** toolbar button. PowerPoint displays the Apply Design Template dialog box, which contains a list of available color schemes.

WHY WORRY?

If your list of design templates looks different from the list here, you may not have all the templates installed on your computer. Reinstall Microsoft PowerPoint, and then look in the Apply Design Template dialog box again for more templates.

2 When you click the name of a design template, a preview of it appears in the box to the right of the list. Although the sample does not display your text, the design, patterns, and text color and styles show you exactly what you'll see in slides. Click the name of the design template you want to use and click **Apply**.

NOTE ▼

If the Presentation Designs folder is not listed in the Look in text box, click the arrow on the Look in drop-down list and select Presentation Designs.

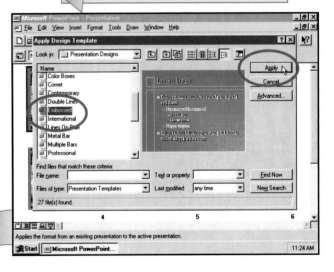

3 PowerPoint returns you to the view you were in before and applies the template's styles to your slides. (PowerPoint applies the new design template to all the thumbnails if you're in Slide Sorter view.) ■

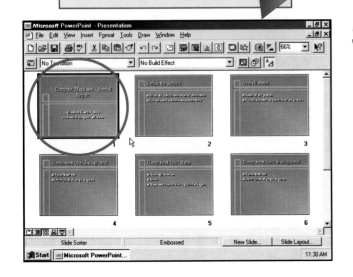

TASK 5
Adding a New Slide

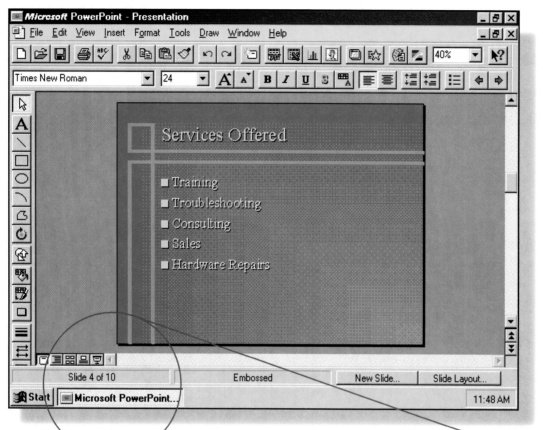

"Why would I do this?"

No matter how thoroughly you plan your presentation, you may forget an important slide and have to add it later. PowerPoint makes it easy to add a slide; in fact, it helps you choose the design you want by giving you a list of choices called *AutoLayouts*. AutoLayouts make it simple to add the type of slide you want to your presentation. Each AutoLayout puts your text in a great location, so all you have to do to enter text is click and type.

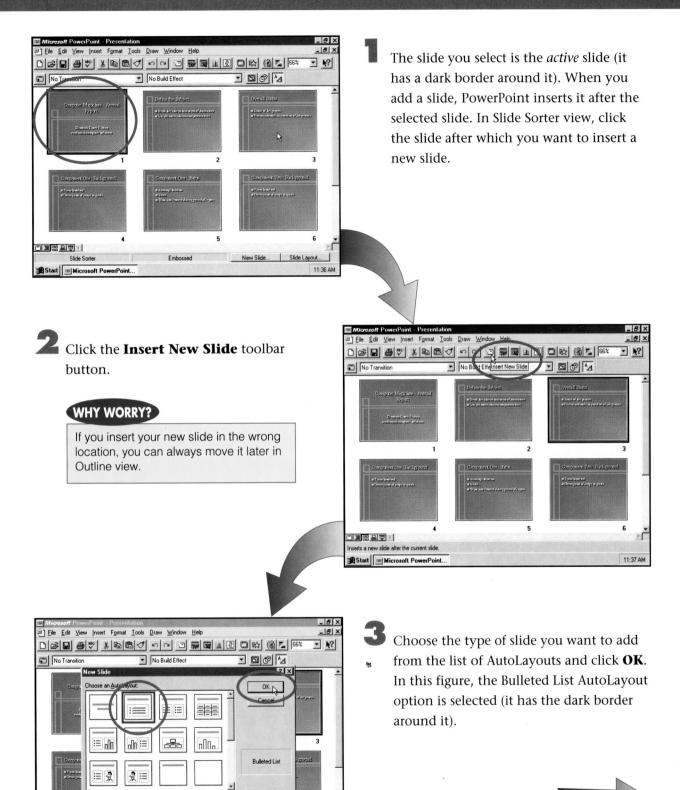

1 The slide you select is the *active* slide (it has a dark border around it). When you add a slide, PowerPoint inserts it after the selected slide. In Slide Sorter view, click the slide after which you want to insert a new slide.

2 Click the **Insert New Slide** toolbar button.

WHY WORRY?

If you insert your new slide in the wrong location, you can always move it later in Outline view.

3 Choose the type of slide you want to add from the list of AutoLayouts and click **OK**. In this figure, the Bulleted List AutoLayout option is selected (it has the dark border around it).

4 PowerPoint adds the new slide to your presentation with all the other slides. Right now, the slide has no text on it. Click the **Slide View** button to switch to a view in which you can add text to the slide.

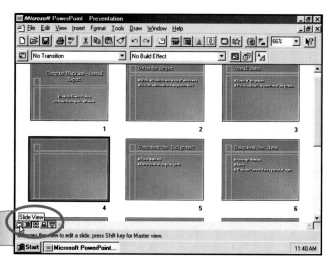

5 Placeholders appear on the slide to show you where to add text. The outline around each placeholder lets you know the amount of space you have for your text. You'll learn how to change the size of the placeholder boxes later.

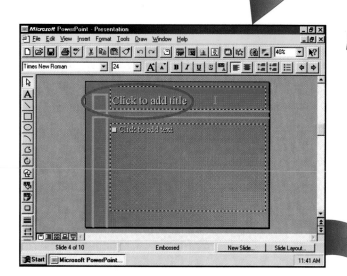

NOTE ▼

You can resize and move placeholder boxes. PowerPoint determines the position of each placeholder based on the selected design template and the AutoLayout you select for the slide.

6 Click the Click to add title placeholder and type the text for the slide's title. Press **Enter** to create a line space in the title. (Pressing Enter does not take you to the next placeholder.) When entering your text, you can use the Backspace and Delete keys to correct any mistakes.

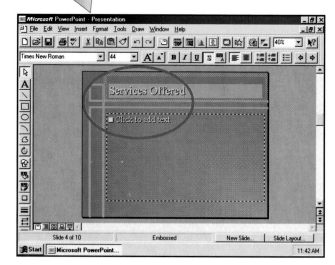

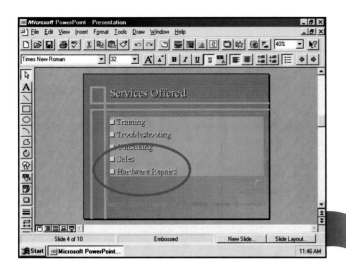

 Click the `Click to add text` placeholder to add the bulleted text. After each bulleted item, press **Enter** to advance to the next bulleted line.

WHY WORRY?

Don't feel like you have to fill in every placeholder box on a slide. If you ignore a `Click to...` message, that area of the slide just remains blank.

8 When you finish entering your text, press **Esc** twice to deselect the text box (eliminate the dotted outline). ■

NOTE ▼

A text box that is selected is outlined with a dotted line or a box.

TASK 6
Saving a Presentation

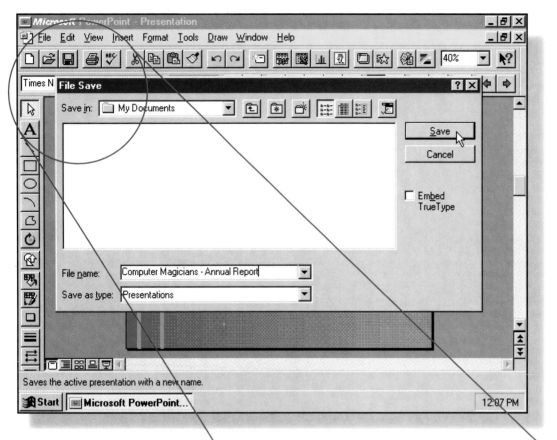

"Why would I do this?"

Few people start a project and work straight through until they finish. If you'd like to be able to work a little at a time on your presentation, you need to save it each time you stop working on it. When you save your work, you must give it a meaningful name and indicate where you want to store it within your computer. Usually, you store it in a specific area where you keep other related work, such as other PowerPoint presentations.

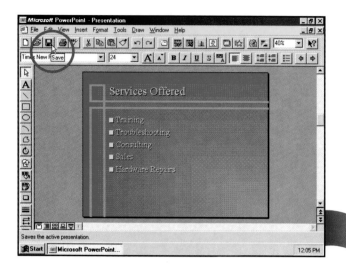

1 PowerPoint displays a presentation's name in the title bar. When you first create a presentation, PowerPoint automatically calls it "Presentation." After you save your presentation, the name you give it appears in the title bar. To save your presentation, click the **Save** button. The File Save dialog box appears.

WHY WORRY?

The File Save dialog box appears only when you save a presentation that has not yet been named.

2 Type a name for your presentation in the **File name** text box. The name can contain up to 255 characters, including spaces and punctuation. When you finish entering the name, click **Save**.

NOTE ▼

If you're creating a presentation that's similar to an existing one, open the existing presentation and click File, Save As. Enter a new name in the File name text box and click Save. PowerPoint creates a new file, and your original file remains unchanged.

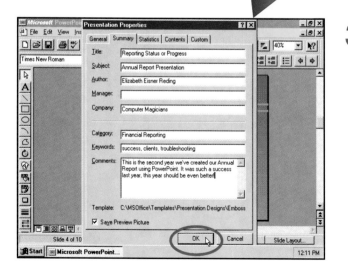

3 You can enter summary information about the presentation in the Presentation Properties dialog box. This information is optional, but it adds important details about your presentation. Enter the information you want to record and click **OK**. (Depending on how PowerPoint is installed on your computer, this dialog box may not appear. If it doesn't, PowerPoint returns you to the active slide after step 2.) ■

Printing a Presentation

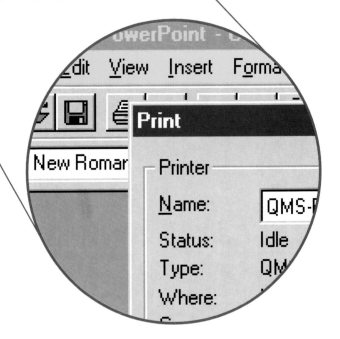

"Why would I do this?"

Even though you create your presentation electronically and plan to show your slides using a computer, you may want to print out a hard copy of your work. In each of its views, PowerPoint enables you to print your slides individually or to print handouts that include thumbnails of all the slides in a presentation on a single page. You can then pass the hard copies on to anyone who couldn't sit in on your presentation.

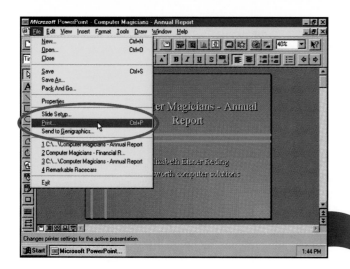

1 Open the **File** menu and choose **Print** to access the Print dialog box, in which you can choose the type of printed materials you want.

NOTE ▼

If you click the Print button on the Standard toolbar (the one with the picture of a printer on it), PowerPoint automatically prints one copy of the open presentation in the current view. So if you have a presentation open in Slide view and you click the Print button, you'll get one copy of each slide in that presentation.

2 In the Print dialog box, you choose the slides you want to print and how many copies you want. You can print a presentation in a view other than the one that's currently displayed on-screen by clicking on the **Print what** drop-down arrow and selecting from the choices listed. To change the number of copies that print, change the number in the **Number of Copies** box.

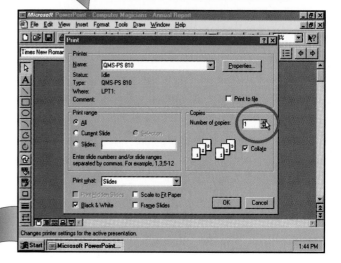

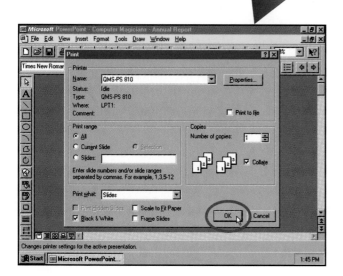

3 When you finish making your selections, click **OK**. ■

WHY WORRY?

You can stop a print job you've started by double-clicking the printer symbol (or *icon*) on the status bar. A red X appears over the icon, and PowerPoint deletes the print job.

Closing a Presentation

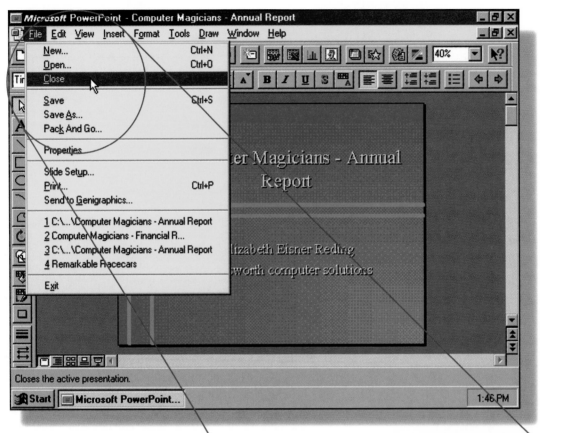

"Why would I do this?"

Closing a presentation when you finish working on it frees up memory in your computer. Your computer uses this memory to perform a variety of Windows 95 and PowerPoint tasks. In addition, if you close a presentation, you don't run the risk of accidentally making changes to it.

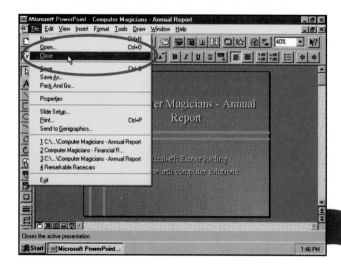

1 Open the **File** menu and choose **Close**. If you haven't made any changes to your presentation since you opened it or since the last time you saved it, PowerPoint automatically closes the file.

2 If you have made changes since the last time you saved the file, PowerPoint asks you if you want to save the changes now. Choose **Yes** to save the changes. (You can choose No to abandon the changes or Cancel to return to the presentation.)

NOTE ▼

If you choose to save changes to an unnamed presentation, PowerPoint displays the File Save dialog box so you can name the file.

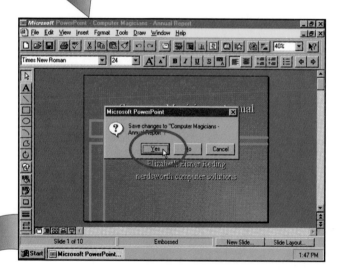

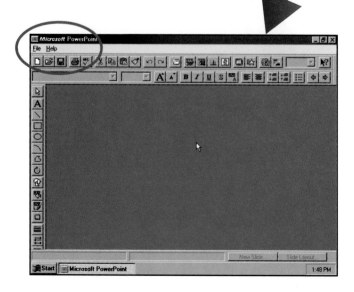

3 When PowerPoint closes your presentation, it displays only the File and Help menus on-screen. From here, you can start a new file, open an existing one, or exit the program. ■

Starting a New Presentation

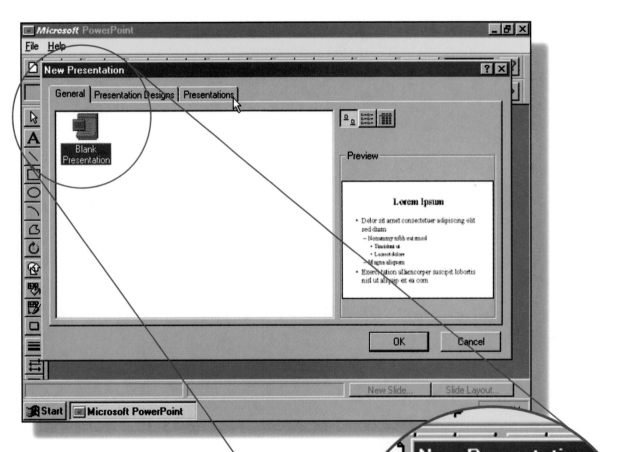

"Why would I do this?"

If you don't want to use the AutoContent Wizard to create a new presentation, you have an alternative. PowerPoint comes with a variety of predesigned slide shows. These slide shows include text and design templates for many topics. You can use them as they are, or you can modify them to suit your needs.

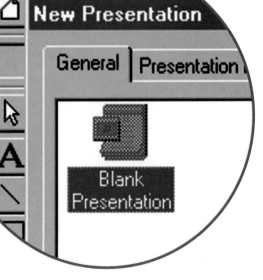

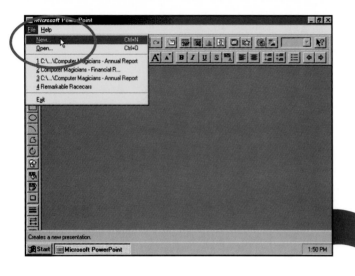

1 Open the **File** menu and choose **New** to start a new presentation or to select of one of the predesigned presentations.

2 To use a predesigned presentation, choose the **Presentations** tab and click **OK**. (You can start from scratch by selecting the **Blank Presentation** icon on the General tab.)

WHY WORRY?

If you don't see a predesigned presentation you think you can use, you can start the AutoContent Wizard from the Presentations tab. Click the AutoContent Wizard icon, and PowerPoint starts the AutoContent Wizard (see Task 2).

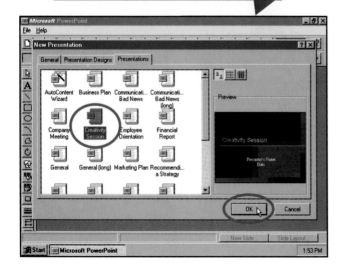

3 In the Presentations tab, click the icon for the type of presentation you want to create and click **OK**. ■

NOTE ▼

You can browse through the predesigned presentations to see what they're like. When you click on an icon, PowerPoint displays a preview of that presentation type on the right side of the dialog box.

31

Opening an Existing Presentation

"Why would I do this?"

Most of us have more than one project to work on at a time. Because you save your files on your computer's hard disk or on a floppy disk, you can open an existing presentation file so you can work on it again.

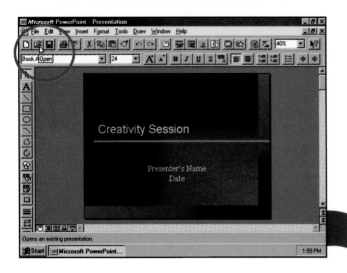

1 Click the **Open** button on the Standard toolbar. The File Open dialog box appears.

2 Choose the name of the file you want to open from the Name list and click **Open**. A thumbnail of the selected file appears so you can see if it's the right file.

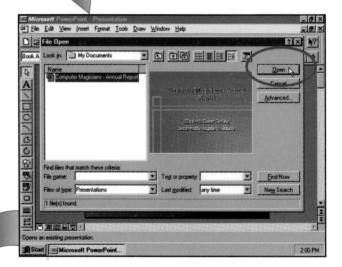

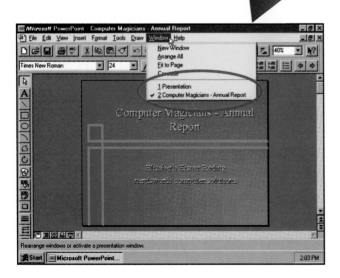

3 The presentation you selected appears on the screen. ■

TASK 11
Getting Help

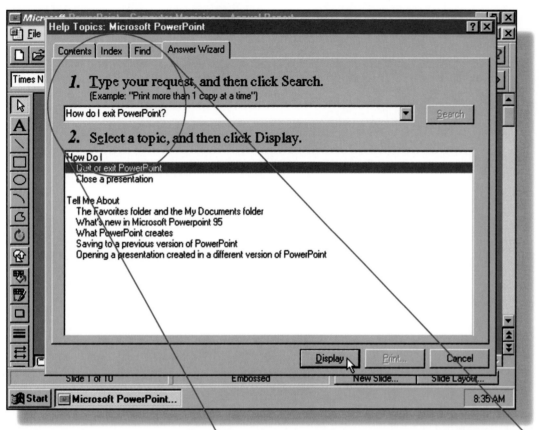

"Why would I do this?"

When you run up against a wall and can't figure out how to perform a task in PowerPoint, you can access the program's online Help system. PowerPoint's Help system gives you a variety of ways to find the information you need. Not only does Help find the information for you, but it automatically displays the appropriate steps on your screen! The Help window contains four tabs (which you use to find information about how to perform specific tasks) as well as general information about the program.

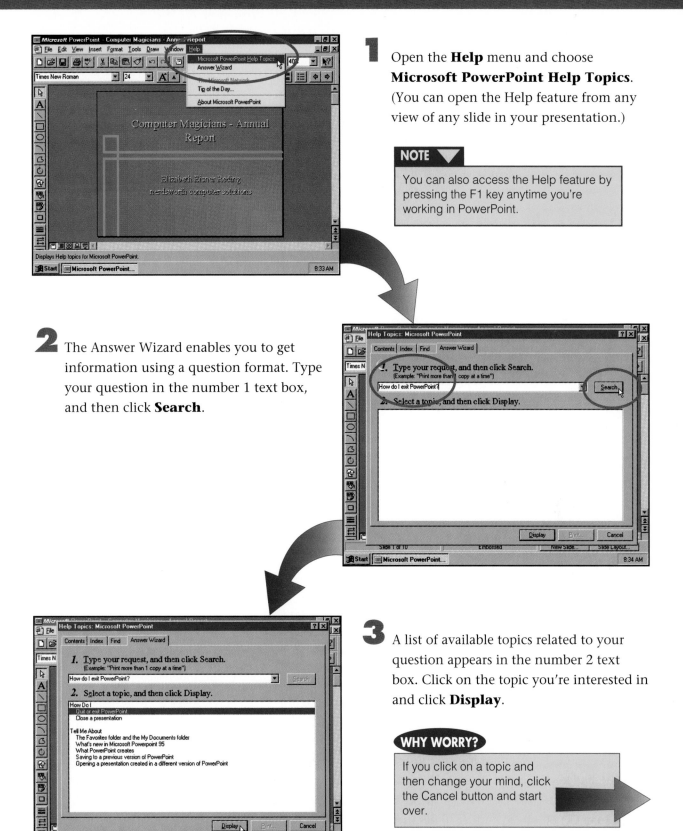

1 Open the **Help** menu and choose **Microsoft PowerPoint Help Topics**. (You can open the Help feature from any view of any slide in your presentation.)

NOTE ▼

You can also access the Help feature by pressing the F1 key anytime you're working in PowerPoint.

2 The Answer Wizard enables you to get information using a question format. Type your question in the number 1 text box, and then click **Search**.

3 A list of available topics related to your question appears in the number 2 text box. Click on the topic you're interested in and click **Display**.

WHY WORRY?

If you click on a topic and then change your mind, click the Cancel button and start over.

4 Click the **Next** button in the Answer Wizard dialog box. What appears next depends on the Help topic you've chosen. Regardless, the Answer Wizard takes over your screen and shows you exactly which commands you need to use in order to complete the selected task.

WHY WORRY?

If you misspell the subject you want information on, press the Backspace key and retype it.

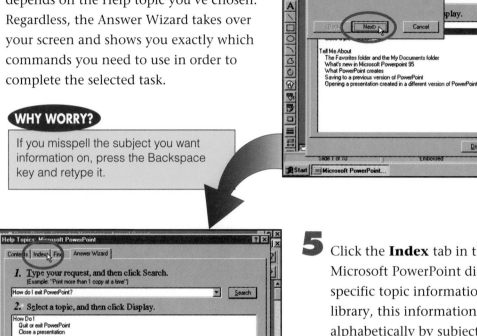

5 Click the **Index** tab in the Help Topics: Microsoft PowerPoint dialog box to locate specific topic information. As it is in a library, this information is organized alphabetically by subject.

NOTE ▼

The Question mark button in the upper-right corner of a dialog box gives you access to additional information on a topic. Click this button and then click a topic, menu item, or button, and PowerPoint displays specific Help information about whatever you selected.

6 In the number 1 text box, type the first few characters of the subject you want information on, and related topics appear in the number 2 text box. Select the topic you're interested in and click **Display**. Whenever possible, the Answer Wizard takes over and supplies information. Press the **Esc** key when the Answer Wizard finishes. If a Help dialog box appears, click the **Close** (X) box in the upper-right corner. ■

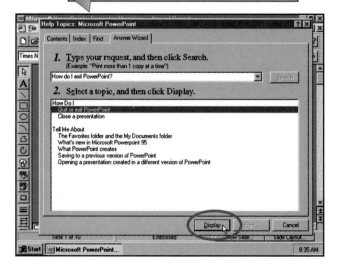

Exiting Microsoft PowerPoint

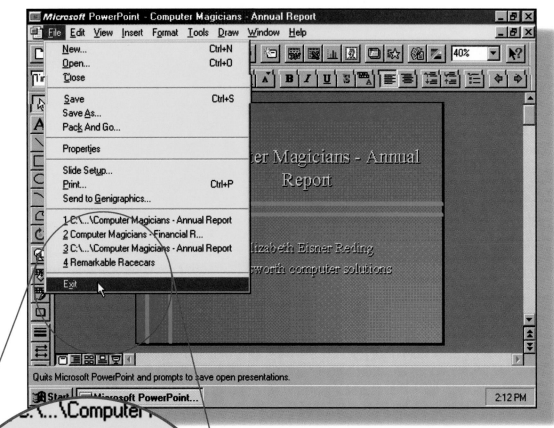

"Why would I do this?"

When you finish working in PowerPoint, you need to leave the program. Correctly exiting any program means learning the right way to exit; if you just turn off the computer when you finish working, you lose any unsaved data and run the risk of damaging other files.

1 Open the **File** menu and choose **Exit**. If you haven't made changes to any open files since the last time you saved them, PowerPoint closes the open files and shuts down the program.

> **NOTE** ▼
>
> You can switch from one open file to another by clicking a file name in the Window menu.

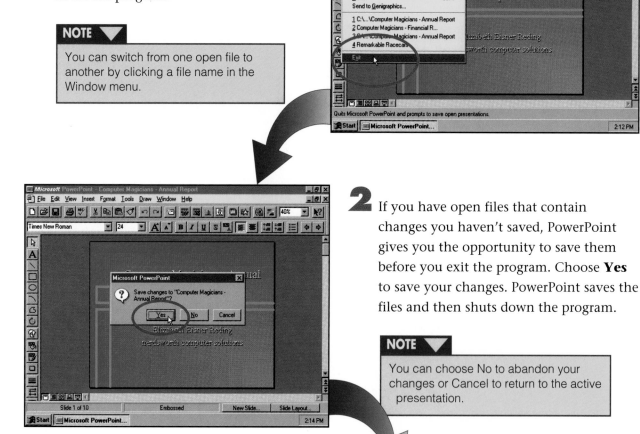

2 If you have open files that contain changes you haven't saved, PowerPoint gives you the opportunity to save them before you exit the program. Choose **Yes** to save your changes. PowerPoint saves the files and then shuts down the program.

> **NOTE** ▼
>
> You can choose No to abandon your changes or Cancel to return to the active presentation.

3 From the Windows 95 desktop, you can continue working on other programs or shut down your computer. To shut down the computer, click the **Start** button on the taskbar, point to **Shut Down**, click **Shut down the computer?**, and click **Yes**. In a minute or two, you see the message It's now safe to turn off your computer. When you see that message, turn off the computer. ■

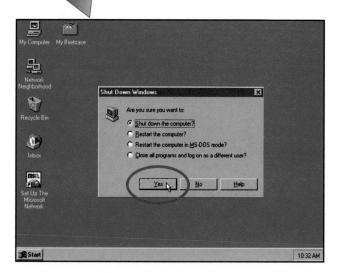

PART II
Working with Text

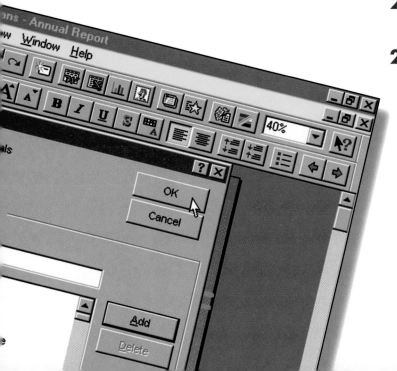

Bold

Italic

Underline

Because PowerPoint makes it so easy to create powerful presentations, you can spend more time working with your text to make it sound and look its best.

No matter how much time you spend planning your presentation, you're bound to forget something. Luckily, adding, editing, and deleting text from a slide is easy. You can copy and paste text you select using the Windows Clipboard, and you can delete selected text by pressing the Delete key. In addition, you can move text simply by *dragging* it with your mouse from one spot to another. And because you can cut, copy, and paste information already in your slides, you spend less time typing and more time making your presentation great.

One of the most important tools included in PowerPoint is its spell checking utility. It would be a shame to ruin a beautiful presentation with typographical errors. The spell checking utility checks the text in your slides against its built-in dictionary. Even though the dictionary contains a tremendous number of words, you can personalize your PowerPoint dictionary by adding to it any words you use frequently. That way, the spelling checker doesn't tell you a word is misspelled when you know that it is spelled correctly.

In case you forget to use the spelling checker, PowerPoint automatically checks your spelling for commonly misspelled or mistyped words (such as *teh* for *the*) using a feature called AutoCorrect. As you type text on your slides, the AutoCorrect feature compares each word you type with words on the AutoCorrect list to correct the typos you make the most. When it finds a word on the list, it automatically makes the correction—without even telling you! And just as you can with the spell checking utility, you can personalize the AutoCorrect list, adding words you often have trouble with.

PowerPoint's AutoLayout feature already contains formatting *attributes* such as boldface, italics, underlining, and shadowing that affect every slide you see in your presentation. However, you might want to add emphasis to specific words within your slides. Toolbar buttons make it easy for you to add these enhancements whenever you choose.

Not only can you enhance your text with formatting attributes, but you can change the appearance of the text (called the *font*) you use in your slides as well as the size of the individual characters. Every computer has different fonts installed on it, and almost all computers have the fonts Times New Roman, Futura, and Helvetica. Fonts come in two basic types: serif and sans serif. A *serif* is an edge found on letters such as s, a, l, and r that makes words easier to distinguish visually; therefore, people commonly use serif fonts in bodies of text. Times New Roman is a serif font. A *sans serif* font has no edges on its characters, which gives it a smoother, cleaner appearance. People often use sans serif fonts for titles, headlines, captions, and other shorter passages of text. Futura is an example of a sans serif font.

The following table shows you samples of some common fonts and tells you the best way to use them to enhance your presentation text.

Commonly Used Fonts

Font Name	Serif/Sans Serif	Best Use
Futura	Sans serif	Titles, headlines, or captions
Helvetica	Sans serif	Titles, headlines, or captions
Times New Roman	Serif	Bodies of text or bulleted items
AGaramond	Serif	Bodies of text or bulleted items

It's fun to use fonts to dress up your slides, but it's important to remember not to use too many fonts on one slide. The general rule of thumb is to use no more than two fonts per slide. The reason for this is that one additional font calls attention to itself, whereas two additional fonts detract from each other and the original font. And because slides need to be readable to be effective, you don't want to undermine your presentation by using too many fonts.

You can choose whether you want text left-, right-, or center-aligned in titles or in bulleted lists. And you can customize the bullets in a list so they look exactly the way you want them to. A number of symbol fonts (Wingdings, Zapf Dingbats, Symbol, and Monotype Sorts, for example) are available for that purpose. Experiment with them to find unique bullet shapes.

In this part of the book, you learn how to manipulate the text in your slides by changing its appearance or location.

Editing Existing Text

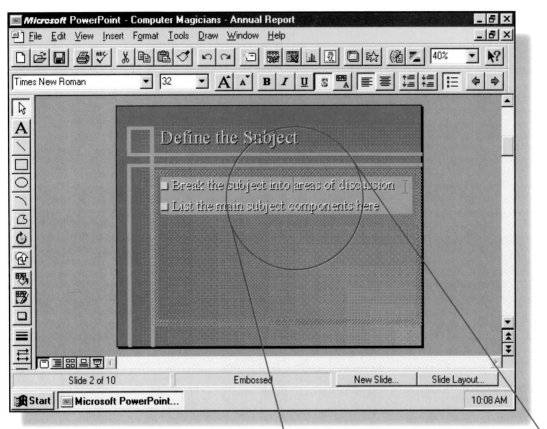

"Why would I do this?"

When you look at your slides, you may find errors in your text, or you may just decide you want to make changes to the text. To edit existing text, you must first activate the text block (it becomes surrounded by a hatched outline). Then you place the cursor in the spot where you want to edit the text, and you make changes just as you would in a word processor.

1 Click anywhere within the block containing the text you want to change to select the block. The mouse pointer changes to an I-beam, and a hatched outline surrounds the text block. Click in the location you want to edit, and the *insertion point* (the I-beam) appears there. Press **Delete** to remove characters to the right, press **Backspace** to remove characters to the left, or simply enter any text you want to add.

2 After you make your changes, press the **Esc** key twice or click outside of the selected text block. The hatched outline surrounding the text block disappears, and PowerPoint returns you to the slide. ■

NOTE ▼

As you make changes to text on a slide, PowerPoint automatically moves your words so they wrap around at the end of each line.

WHY WORRY?

If you delete a character accidentally, open the Edit menu and select Undo, and the character reappears.

45

Deleting Text

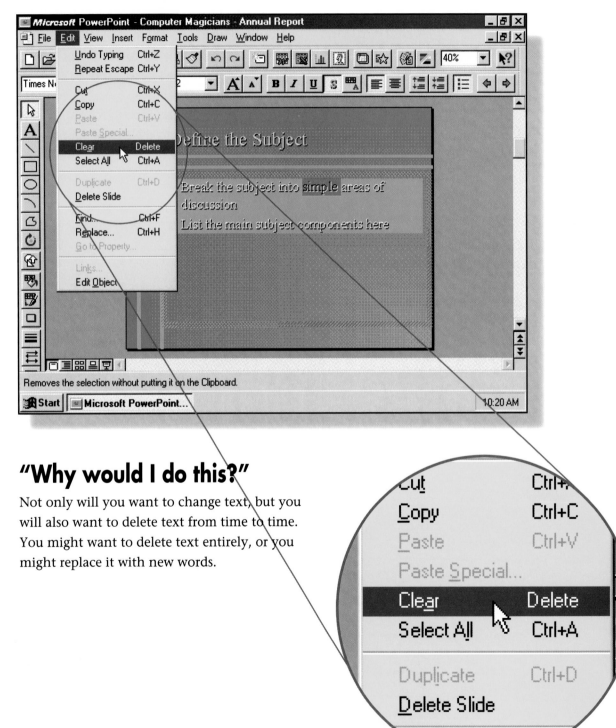

"Why would I do this?"

Not only will you want to change text, but you will also want to delete text from time to time. You might want to delete text entirely, or you might replace it with new words.

1 Click the block containing the text you want to delete, and then double-click on the word you want to delete to select it. When you select text, its background turns to a different color. You can select a group of words by clicking the mouse button on the first word and dragging until all the words you want are highlighted.

NOTE ▼

Another way to select a group of words is to click to the left of the first word, hold down the Shift key, and click to the right of the last word.

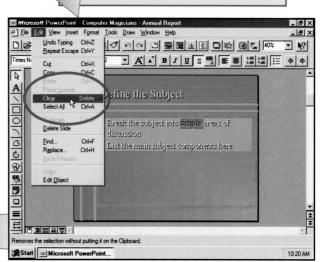

2 When you've selected the words you want to delete, open the **Edit** menu and select **Clear**, or press the **Delete** key.

3 The selected words disappear, and PowerPoint rewraps the text to fill in the spot where you deleted the words. ■

WHY WORRY?

If you delete characters accidentally, open the Edit menu and select Undo, and the characters reappear.

Moving a Text Block

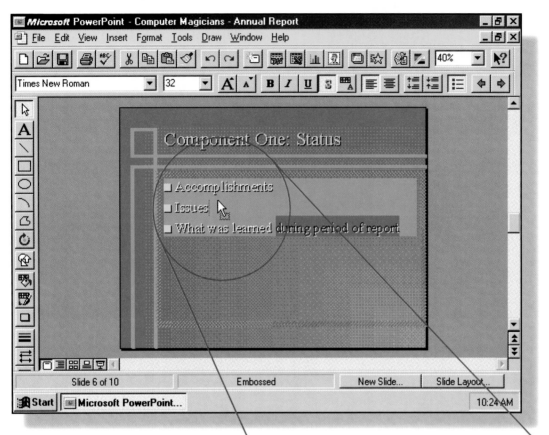

"Why would I do this?"

Suppose you just typed some really excellent text, only to realize it's in the wrong place. Your first impulse is to delete the text and start typing it again where you want it—but you don't have to do that. PowerPoint has a handy feature called drag-and-drop that enables you to use your mouse to move text from one place to another.

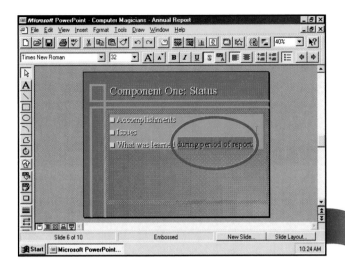

1 Select the appropriate text block, and then select the text you want to move. PowerPoint highlights the text.

2 Position the mouse pointer over the selected text, press and hold down the left mouse button, and drag the text to its new location.

NOTE ▼

When you drag the mouse pointer, you don't actually see the selected text move; instead, you see a square under the mouse pointer that represents the text you are moving.

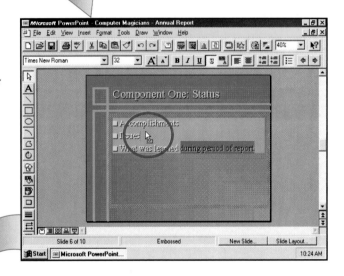

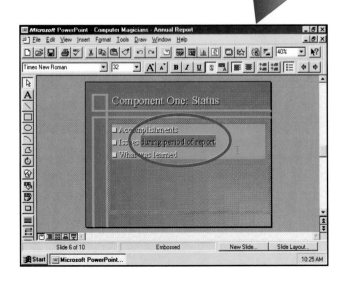

3 When the pointer is in the new location, release the mouse button. PowerPoint "drops" the selected text in the new location (removing it from its original location). ∎

WHY WORRY?

If you move text to the wrong location, you can select the Edit, Undo command, or you can drag and drop the text again.

Cutting, Copying, and Pasting Text

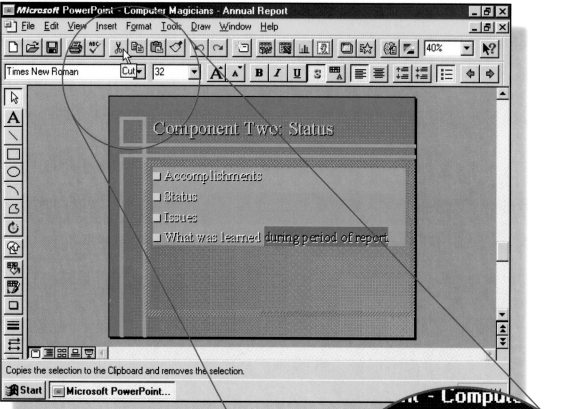

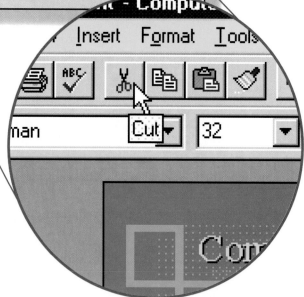

"Why would I do this?"

You can save yourself a lot of time—and typing—by cutting or copying existing text and pasting it in a new location. You can paste cut or copied text in the same slide or in another slide. When you cut text, PowerPoint duplicates it and removes it from the original location (see steps 1 and 2). When you copy text, PowerPoint duplicates it and leaves the original intact (see steps 3–5). If you hate typing or you're in a hurry, the ability to cut, copy, and paste text is a real lifesaver!

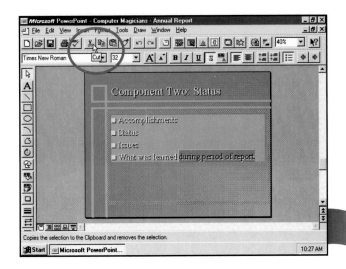

1 Select the text you want to cut and click on the **Cut** button. PowerPoint places the selected text in the Clipboard and removes it from its original location.

NOTE ▼

The *Clipboard* is a temporary storage area. Although you don't actually see the Clipboard, it holds a copy of only the last block of text you cut or copied. If you cut one block of text and then cut another, the second block of text overwrites the first block in the Clipboard.

2 Click in the location where you want to place the cut text, and then click the **Paste** button. PowerPoint inserts the text from the Clipboard in that location.

NOTE ▼

The cut and paste process achieves the same result as the drag-and-drop feature (explained in Task 15).

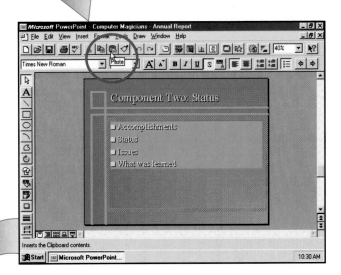

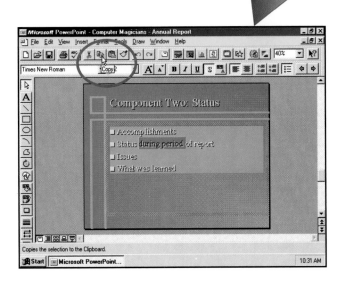

3 To copy text, select the text you want to copy and click on the **Copy** button. The original text stays where it is, and PowerPoint places a copy of it in the Clipboard.

WHY WORRY?

You can use the contents of the Clipboard more than once without having to recopy the information. Just click the Paste button to paste the text as many times as you need to.

4 Insert the I-beam where you want to place the copied text. Then click on the **Paste** button.

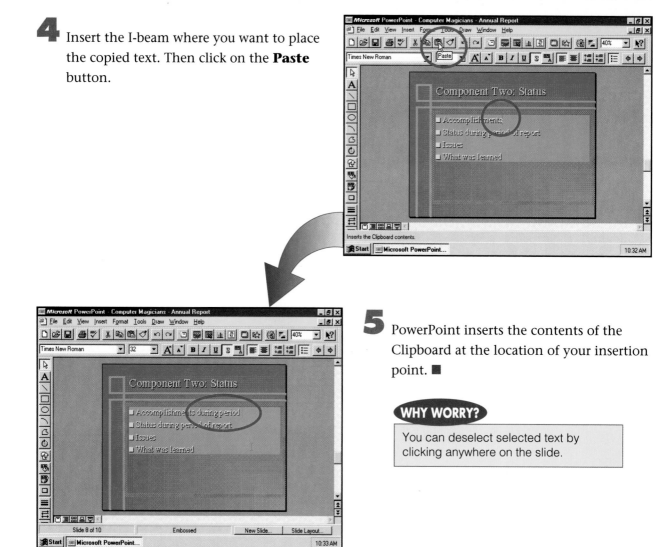

5 PowerPoint inserts the contents of the Clipboard at the location of your insertion point. ∎

WHY WORRY?

You can deselect selected text by clicking anywhere on the slide.

Checking Spelling

"Why would I do this?"

Everyone makes typographical and spelling errors at one time or another. But it would be a shame to let these errors ruin a beautiful presentation. Fortunately, PowerPoint's spell checking utility and built-in dictionary make it easy to find and fix them. PowerPoint even enables you to add your own words to its built-in dictionary.

1 Click the **Spelling** button to start the spell checking utility, which compares words in your presentation to words in its dictionary.

NOTE ▼

You can check the spelling of one word or a group of words by selecting the text you want to check *before* you click the Spelling button. If you don't select any text, the spell checking utility checks the entire presentation.

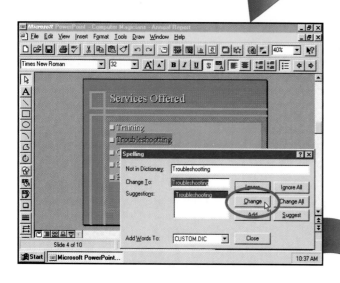

2 When the spell checking utility finds a word in your text that doesn't match any words in the dictionary, it displays the misspelled word and other suggested spellings in the Spelling dialog box. Click **Change** to change the word to the selected suggestion. (Alternatively, click Change All to change all occurrences of the misspelled word, click Ignore to leave the word the way it is, or click Ignore All to leave all occurrences of the word.)

3 Even if you spell a word correctly, if it is not in PowerPoint's dictionary, the spelling checker flags it. If you use the word frequently (your company name, for example), click the **Add** button to add it to the dictionary so the spell checking utility will not flag it as a misspelled word. ■

WHY WORRY?

If you need to stop the spelling utility before it finishes, click the Close button.

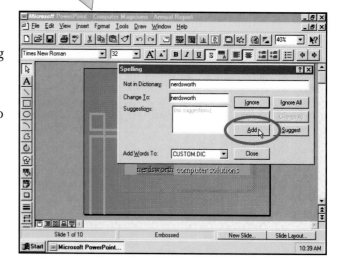

Using AutoCorrect

"Why would I do this?"

The AutoCorrect feature actually checks your words as you type and corrects them without even telling you. You can add your own words to AutoCorrect or delete words already in the list. Use this feature to correct words you misspell often, or be creative and use AutoCorrect as your own "shorthand." For example, you can add your initials to the AutoCorrect list and tell AutoCorrect to replace them with your name automatically.

1 Open the **Tools** menu and choose **AutoCorrect**. The AutoCorrect dialog box appears.

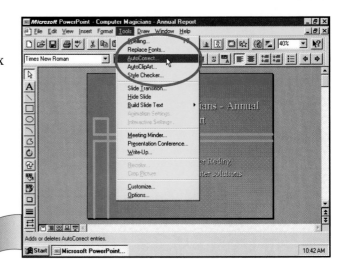

> **NOTE** ▼
>
> Use AutoCorrect to store "shorthand" for words that require a lot of typing. For example, if you often have to type "supercalifragilisticexpialidocious," you can set AutoCorrect to automatically change "super" to the longer word.

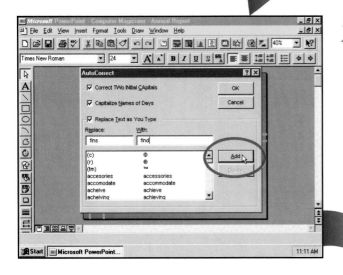

2 In the **Replace** text box, type the word as you often misspell it. In the **With** text box, type the word with which you want to replace the misspelled word. Click **Add** to include this entry in the AutoCorrect list. Add as many entries to the list as you want, and then click **OK**.

3 If you select an entry in the AutoCorrect list or type an entry in the Replace text box that's already in the AutoCorrect list, the Delete button appears. Click **Delete** to delete an entry from the AutoCorrect list. Click **OK** when you finish modifying the AutoCorrect list. ■

> **WHY WORRY?**
>
> To turn off AutoCorrect, click in the Replace Text as You Type check box to remove the check mark. Then click OK.

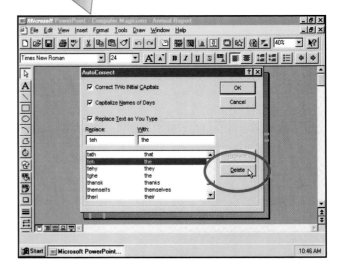

Adding Emphasis to Text

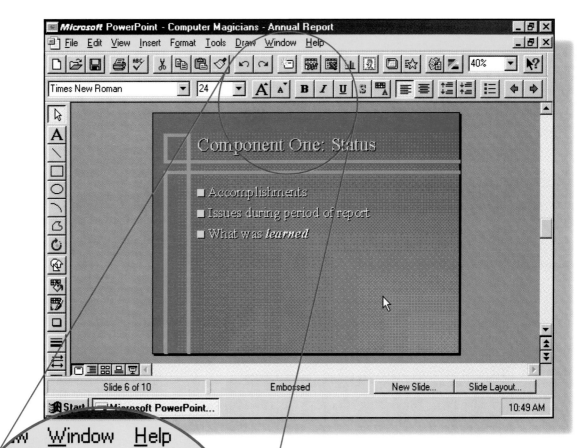

"Why would I do this?"

As you're perfecting the text in your slides, you might decide you want to emphasize some of the words. You can emphasize text by adding attributes such as boldface, italics, underlining, or shadow. You can easily add any of these attributes to text using buttons on the Formatting toolbar.

1 Select the word or words you want to make bold and click the **Bold** button. The selected text appears bold.

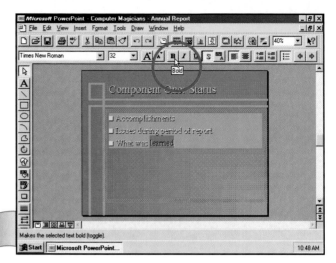

2 Select the word or words you want to italicize and click the **Italic** button. The text appears in italics.

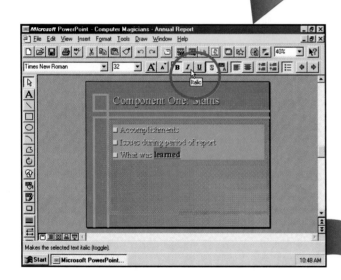

NOTE ▼

When you select a word or character to which one of these attributes is applied, the toolbar button appears to be pushed in.

3 Select the text you want to underline and click the **Underline** button. An underline appears under the word. ■

WHY WORRY?

Attribute buttons like the Bold and Italic buttons are called *toggles*. You click a toggle once to turn the attribute on; you click it again to turn the attribute off. So if you apply an attribute and then change your mind about it, click the toggle button again to turn it off.

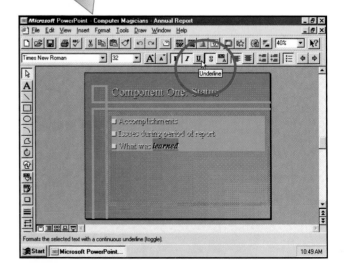

Changing Fonts and Font Sizes

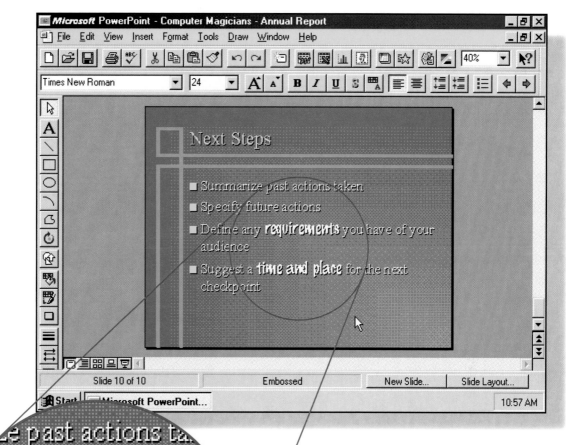

"Why would I do this?"

You might change a font or font size to add emphasis to your text or to create a tone (such as professional or silly) for your document. A *font* is a family of characters that share a similar style and design. Characters within fonts are measured in *points*, and there are 72 points in an inch. The higher the point size, the bigger the character is. You change fonts and font sizes using the Format menu or the Formatting toolbar.

59

1 Select the text whose font you want to change. Open the **Format** menu and choose **Font**. PowerPoint displays the Font dialog box.

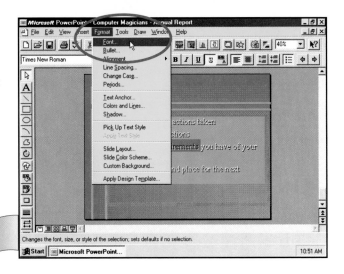

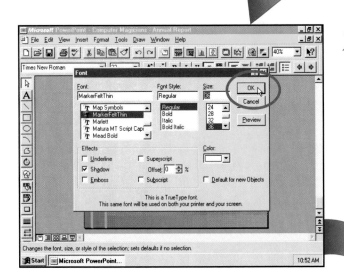

2 Choose a font from the **Font** list, click on attributes in the **Font Style** list, and select a size from the **Size** list. You can add other effects by clicking in the appropriate check boxes in the Effects section. When you finish making changes, click **OK**. The selected text reflects your font changes.

WHY WORRY?

Your list of fonts might look different from the one in this book. Anyone can install additional fonts on her computer, so not all computers have the same fonts available.

3 You can apply fonts directly from the Formatting toolbar by selecting the text you want to change, clicking on the **Font** drop-down arrow, and clicking on the font you want. The new font name appears in the Font list on the Formatting toolbar.

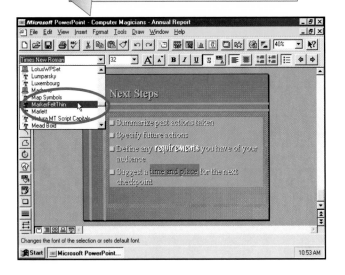

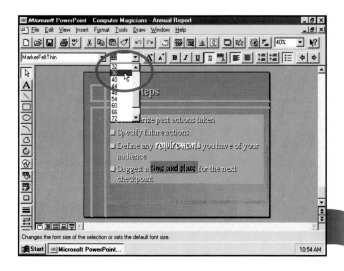

4 You can change the font size from the Formatting toolbar by selecting the text, clicking on the **Font Size** drop-down arrow, and clicking on the size you want.

NOTE ▼

Font sizes appear to vary. For example, 12-point Times New Roman doesn't appear to be the same size as some other 12-point fonts. If you measure the height of the characters, however, the actual point size of the fonts is the same. Some typefaces spread out more than others and appear to be larger or smaller.

5 Although you may not know the precise point size you want, you'll know it when you see it. You can increase the point size of selected text in increments by clicking the **Increase Font Size** button. When you like the result, just leave it.

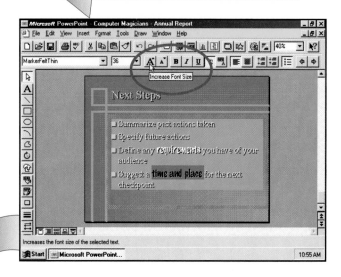

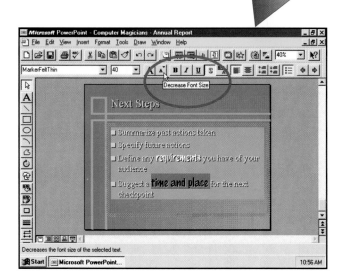

6 Click on the **Decrease Font Size** button to decrease the point size of selected text in increments. This enables you to determine the size you want by making a visual judgment. ■

TASK 21
Aligning Text

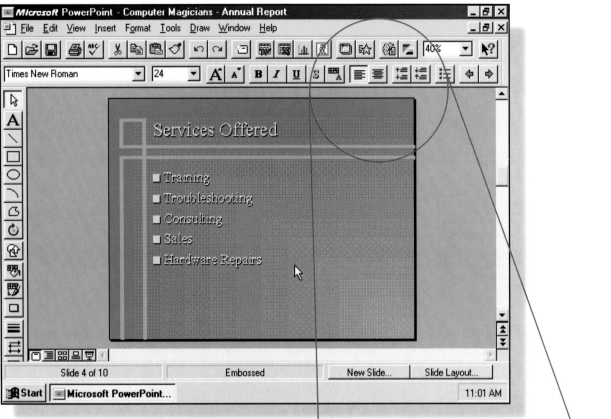

"Why would I do this?"

Part of perfecting your presentation includes
making sure you line up all your text exactly
the way you want it. For example, you can use
text alignment to draw your audience's
attention to a particular part of a slide. You can
align text at the left margin, at the right
margin, or centered between the left and right
margins.

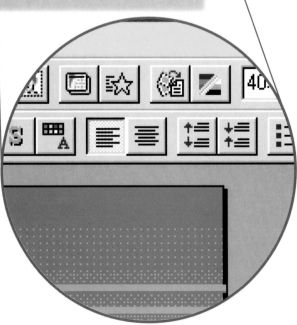

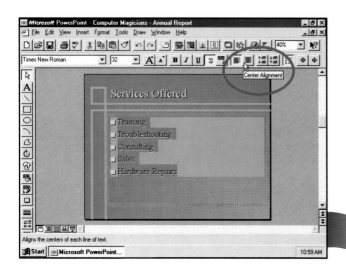

1 To center text, select the text you want to center and click the **Center Alignment** button. PowerPoint centers the text between the margins of the text block.

2 To change the alignment of the selected text and make it flush with the right margin, open the **Format** menu, choose **Alignment**, and choose **Right**. PowerPoint aligns all the text at the right margin.

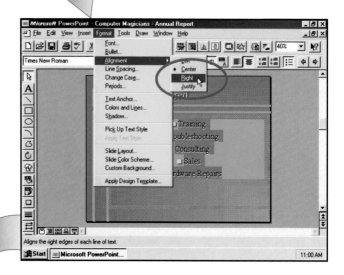

3 To align the selected text with the left margin, click the **Left Alignment** button on the Formatting toolbar. PowerPoint aligns all the text at the left margin. ■

WHY WORRY?

If you like the alignment within a text block but you want to move the text, click on the hatched border, hold down the mouse button, and drag the block to a new location.

63

Modifying a Bullet Symbol

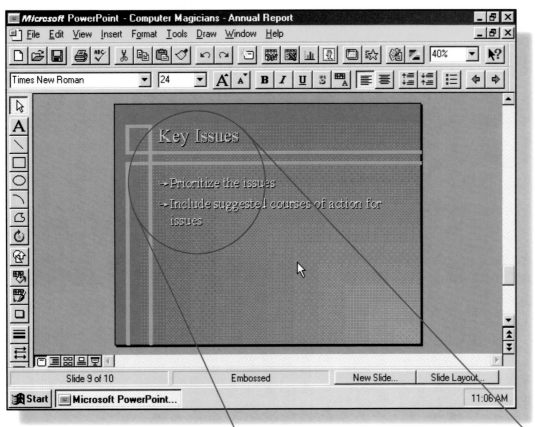

"Why would I do this?"

Each design template uses a certain bullet symbol in front of indented text. However, you might want to change the bullet symbol in order to call attention to it or to make it fit the theme of your presentation. Changing the bullet symbol is easy and fun.

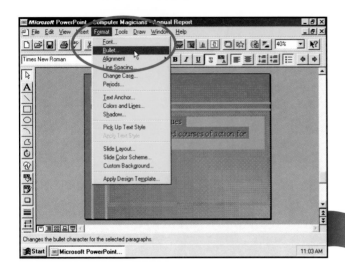

1 Select the bulleted lines of text for which you want to change the bullet symbol. Open the **Format** menu andchoose **Bullet**. The Bullet dialog box appears.

WHY WORRY?

Symbols, like fonts, are installed on computers on an individual basis. If your symbols look different from the ones shown here, you just have different symbols installed.

2 Click on the symbol you want to use for a bullet. If you want to change the size of the symbol *in relation to* the text it's in front of, use the **Size** text box's up and down arrows.

NOTE ▼

Try to use no more than two different bullet symbols on any individual slide; more than two symbols can detract from the slide's appearance and distract your viewer.

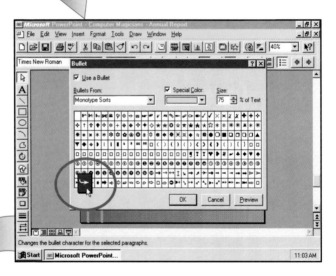

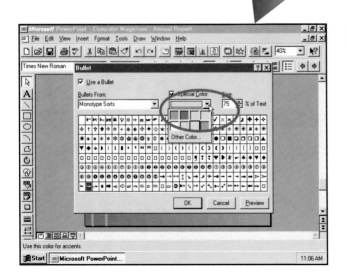

3 You can change the color of the bullet by clicking on the **Special Color** drop-down arrow and selecting a color from the list. When you finish making your selections, click **OK**. PowerPoint makes those changes to the selected bullets. ■

PART III
Working with Artwork

After you write and perfect the text for your presentation, it's time to have some fun jazzing up your slides with artwork. You can place *clip art* (electronic files of predesigned art) directly on your slides. Of course, artwork can add more than entertainment value to your slides: it can reinforce your text, show a product, or create a mood for your presentation. Careful use of artwork and color can even "set the tone" of your presentation. For example, if you insert a humorous cartoon instead of a serious picture, it lets your audience know you want them to laugh, relax, and enjoy the presentation. Of course, you probably don't want every piece of artwork to be funny, but one or two pieces of humorous clip art can put the audience at ease.

Microsoft PowerPoint comes with hundreds of pieces of clip art that you can easily insert on any slide. The Microsoft ClipArt Gallery organizes this clip art into categories for you. The Gallery is easy to use. To find artwork you want, simply open the ClipArt Gallery, and then click on category names and choose from the miniature samples (called *thumbnails*) of the images in each category. Like a real art gallery, the ClipArt Gallery displays the contents of each category so you can view them at a glance. Then you select the image you want to use.

You can insert as many pieces of clip art on a slide as you want. After you insert a piece of clip art, you can move it around on the slide or make it larger or smaller—whatever it takes to make it look "just right." You select clip art just as you do text. However, when you select clip art, tiny rectangles called *handles* appear around the image. These handles enable you to move and resize the image. In addition, you can exclude areas of the image (which is called *cropping*), and you can cut, copy, paste, and delete clip art using techniques similar to those you use when working with text.

And, as if it isn't enough that PowerPoint supplies you with all this wonderful clip art, PowerPoint throws in two bonuses: the ability to change colors and to add other images! You can recolor the objects in a clip art file. For example, you can change a red bird with a black beak into a green bird with a yellow beak. You can also add any clip art you buy separately or scan your own (such as a company logo) to the ClipArt Gallery. The ability to add your own clip art makes the ClipArt Gallery a virtual "one-stop shopping" area for artwork.

Even if your words have punch and your artwork looks spectacular, sometimes you need to add your own personal touch to your slides by adding an arrow or a cartoon balloon with a comment in it. PowerPoint includes a wide variety of drawing tools that enable you to accomplish these things with ease and achieve professional-looking results. In addition, PowerPoint provides a wide variety of commonly used shapes called AutoShapes that you can add to your slides. You can add an AutoShape to your slide and move and resize it. It will look exactly the way you want it to—and you never even have to draw it.

This part of the book shows you how to add and manipulate the artwork on your slides to create professional flair!

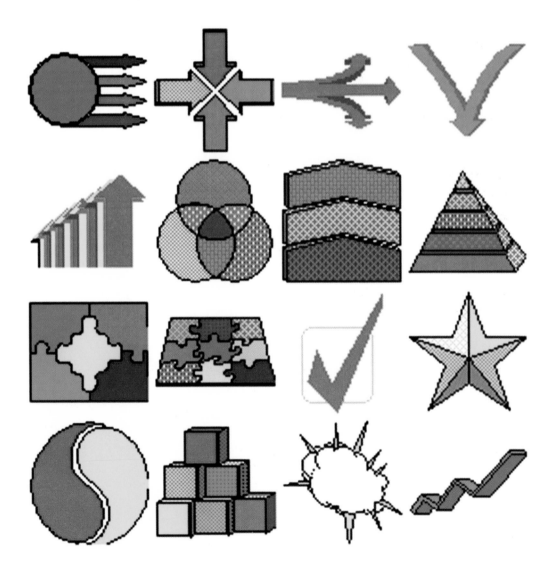

TASK 23
Inserting Clip Art

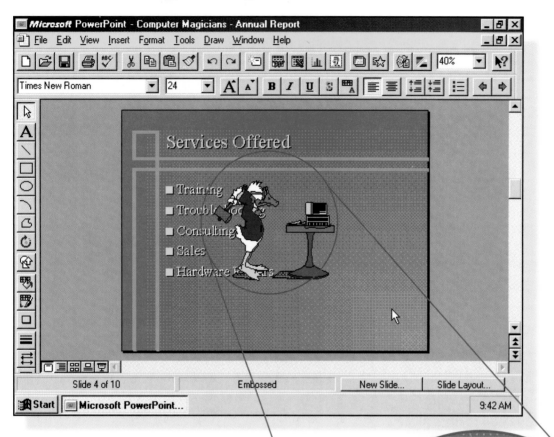

"Why would I do this?"

Artwork makes your slides special. You can add predesigned artwork called *clip art* to your slides to get people's attention, change their moods, or add emphasis to your spoken words. Artwork always dresses up plain-looking slides.

You've heard the expression "a picture is worth a thousand words"? It's true!

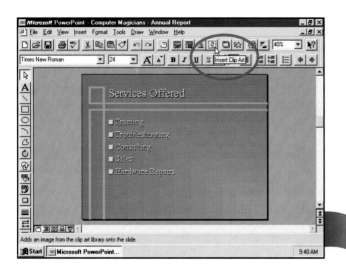

1 With the slide to which you want to add clip art displayed on-screen in Slide View, click the **Insert Clip Art** button on the Standard toolbar.

WHY WORRY?

If you can't find clip art to suit your needs, you can find commercial clip art packages in most computer stores. Many types of electronic artwork are available in file formats that are compatible with PowerPoint.

2 In the Microsoft ClipArt Gallery window, scroll through the available categories in the **Categories** list. The pictures in the selected category appear in the Pictures box. Scroll through the pictures until you find one you want. Click on the desired clip art and click the **Insert** button.

WHY WORRY?

Your Microsoft ClipArt Gallery might contain different images from those shown. Because you can add other files, your computer might have more or less clip art installed.

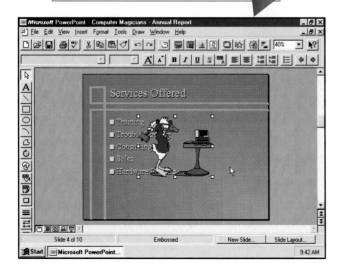

3 The clip art appears on your slide. Black or white squares called *handles* surround the image, indicating that it is selected. Press the **Esc** key to deselect the image. ▪

NOTE ▼

When adding clip art to your slides, you're not limited to using the clip art that came with PowerPoint. You can insert clip art that came with any other program installed on your computer.

Moving Clip Art

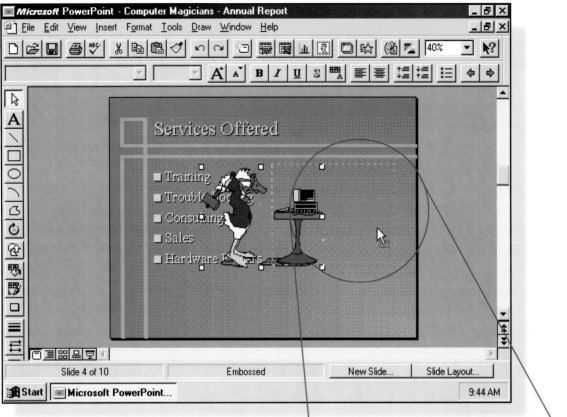

"Why would I do this?"

When you insert clip art on a slide, it rarely appears exactly where you want it. Moving artwork on a slide is as easy as clicking and dragging. By selecting the image and dragging one of its handles, you can place the image exactly where you want it.

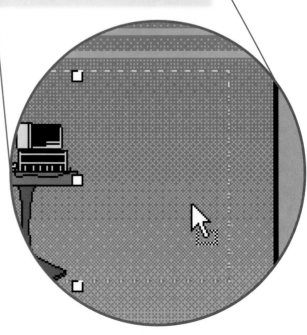

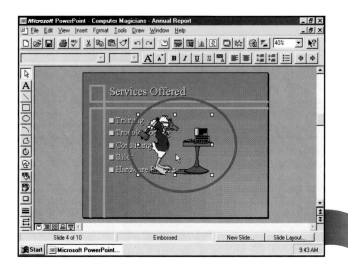

1 When an image is selected, square handles appear all around it. If the image you want to move isn't selected, click on it once to select it.

WHY WORRY?

You absolutely cannot move clip art unless you select the image.

2 Point to one of the handles, press and hold the mouse button, and drag. As you drag, a dotted outline moves with the drag-and-drop pointer. When the dotted outline seems to be in the place you want the image, release the mouse button.

WHY WORRY?

If you select an image accidentally, press the Esc key to deselect it.

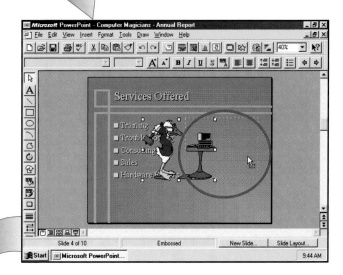

3 The image appears in its new location, still surrounded by handles. If it's not exactly right, click and drag the image as many more times as necessary. When you're satisfied, press the **Esc** key to deselect the image. ■

NOTE ▼

You can simultaneously move more than one piece of artwork on a slide by holding down the Shift key and clicking on each image you want to include.

73

Resizing Clip Art

"Why would I do this?"

When you insert clip art in a slide, it probably won't automatically appear in exactly the size you want. However, you can easily increase or decrease the size of the image using your mouse. For example, if the clip art you insert is so small that it seems lost on your slide, you can increase the size of the image to fill the space you have available.

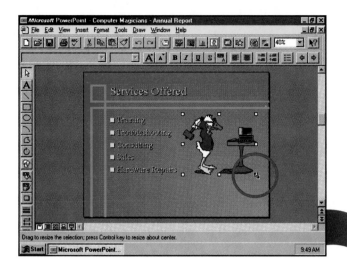

1 If the image is not already surrounded by handles, select it. Then position the mouse pointer on one of the corner handles. The pointer turns into a double-headed diagonal arrow.

2 Hold down the **Ctrl** key, press and hold the mouse button, and drag the mouse. Holding down Ctrl forces PowerPoint to maintain the image's proportions. (Otherwise the duck might look too tall and skinny or short and fat.)

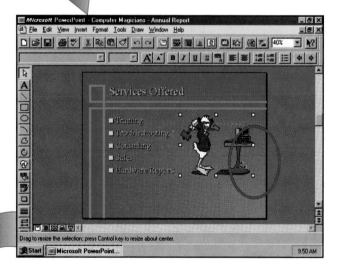

WHY WORRY?

If you use the Ctrl key to preserve the image's proportions, the outline doesn't change until the proportions are accurate; when the image reaches an acceptable dimension, the outline jumps to a new size.

3 When you release the mouse button, PowerPoint displays the image in its new size, surrounded by handles. Press the **Esc** key to deselect the image. ■

Cropping Clip Art

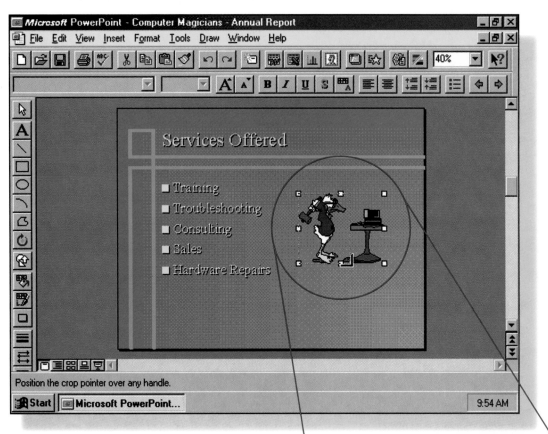

"Why would I do this?"

Suppose you find a nearly perfect piece of artwork, but you don't want one small edge of the image on your slide. You can insert the image into your slide and then crop out the unwanted part. *Cropping* is like placing white paper over unwanted areas of a photograph. Of course, those areas are still there, they're just not visible. Fortunately, in PowerPoint, that hidden area won't appear at all; it's as if the unwanted part never existed!

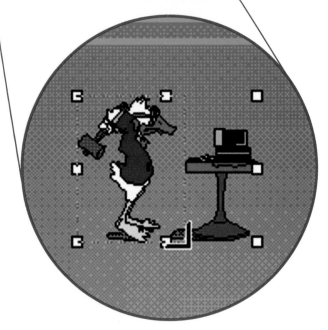

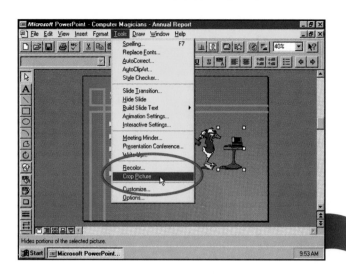

1 Select the image you want to crop, open the **Tools** menu, and choose **Crop Picture**.

2 Place the cropping tool pointer over the handle on the edge of the image you want to crop.

> **NOTE** ▼
>
> You can move or resize a cropped image just as you would any other clip art image (see Tasks 23 and 24).

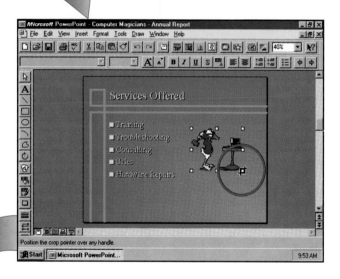

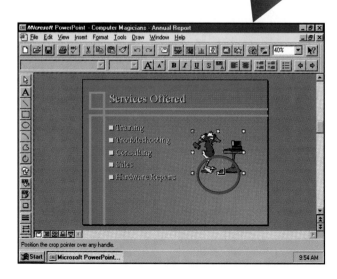

3 Press and hold the mouse button and drag the pointer over the edge you want to hide. You see an outline of the visible image; it shows you how much of the image will remain visible. When the material you want to exclude is no longer visible in the outline, release the mouse button. ■

> **WHY WORRY?**
>
> If you don't crop enough out of an image the first time, repeat these steps until the image is exactly how you want it.

Copying Clip Art

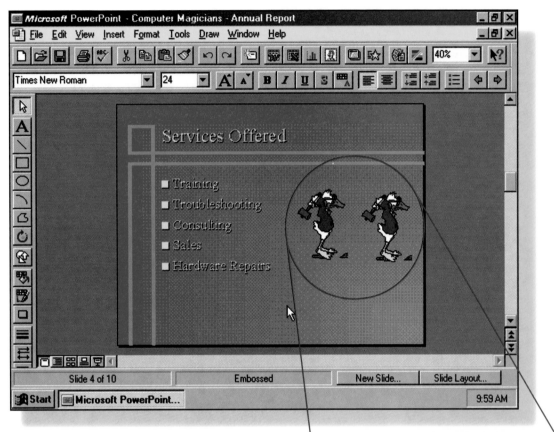

"Why would I do this?"

If you want to use a piece of artwork again, you can always go through the process of inserting it again. However, it's usually easier to copy the image to the Clipboard and paste it in another location. Copying can be especially efficient when you need to reproduce an image that you've already resized or cropped.

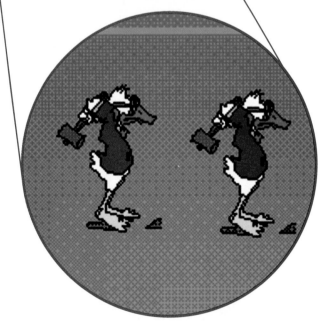

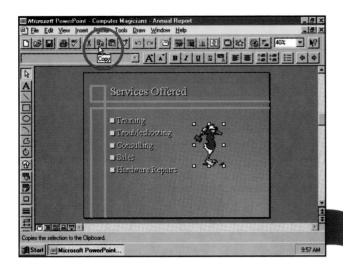

1 Select the image you want to copy and click the **Copy** button on the Standard toolbar.

2 Click the **Paste** button. PowerPoint pastes an identical image on top of the original image. However, the new image is not directly on top of the original; you can see both images. The selection handles appear around the pasted image.

NOTE ▼

You can move, resize, and crop the pasted image just as you would any other image.

3 Position the mouse pointer over the selected image, press and hold the mouse button, and drag the pasted image. An outline of the image moves with the drag-and-drop pointer as you drag. When the outline seems to be where you want it, release the mouse button. ■

WHY WORRY?

If you don't like the way you resized a pasted image, you can always delete it by pressing the Delete key. Then simply paste another copy and try again.

Deleting Clip Art

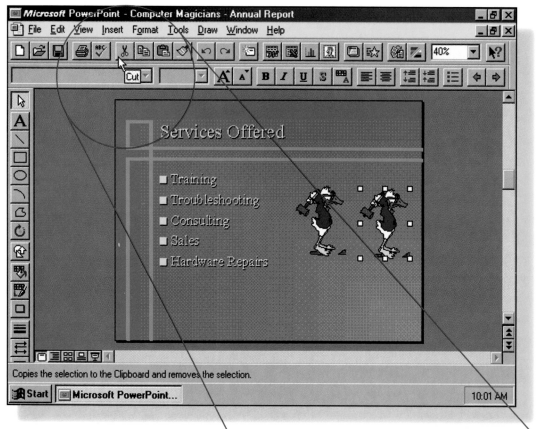

"Why would I do this?"

Even after all your hard work, sometimes a piece of artwork just isn't right, and the only alternative is to delete it. Deleting an image is just like deleting a word: you select the image and click the Cut button or press the Delete key.

1 Select the image you want to delete and click the **Cut** button on the Standard toolbar. When you use the Cut button, PowerPoint places the image in the Clipboard; you can paste the image somewhere else by clicking on the Paste button.

NOTE ▼

You can also delete the image by pressing Delete. When you use the Delete key, PowerPoint *does not* place the image in the Clipboard.

2 The image disappears. You can paste the contents of the Clipboard elsewhere, make another copy of the original, or insert a new piece of clip art. ■

WHY WORRY?

If you delete artwork accidentally, click the Undo button immediately.

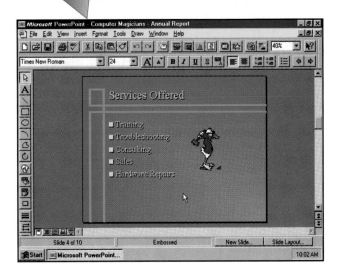

Recoloring Clip Art

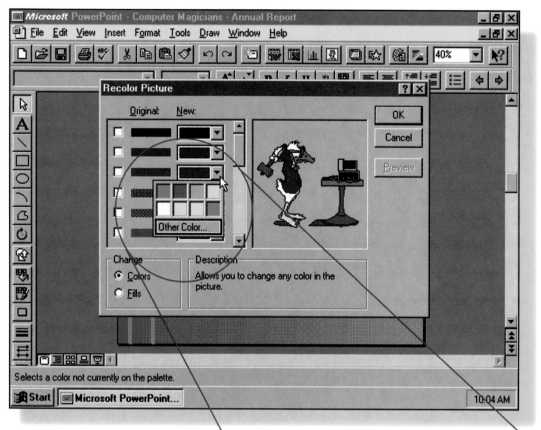

"Why would I do this?"

Suppose you find that "perfect" piece of clip art for a slide, but some of the colors in the image just don't seem right. Well, you're in luck! You can change the colors in most clip art images to make the image look just the way you want it to.

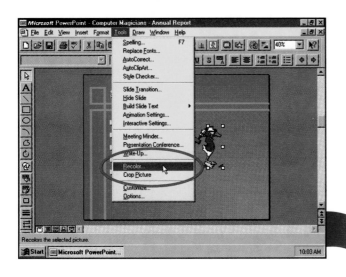

1 Select the image you want to recolor, open the **Tools** menu, and choose **Recolor**.

2 In the Recolor Picture dialog box, PowerPoint shows the image's original colors on the left. Click the arrow to the right of the color you want to change and select a new color.

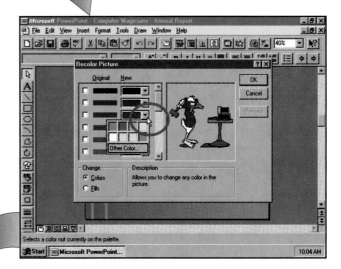

WHY WORRY?

If you don't see a replacement color you like, click the Other Color button. You can choose any color from the huge color palette that appears.

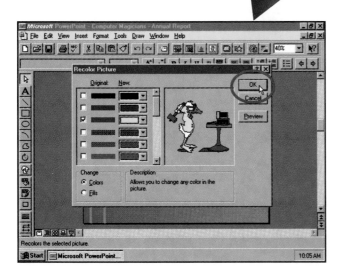

3 In the picture of the selected image, you can see the effects of the changes as you make them. When you're satisfied with your changes, click **OK**. ■

NOTE ▼

You can recolor an image as many times as you want by repeating these steps.

Adding Clip Art to the Gallery

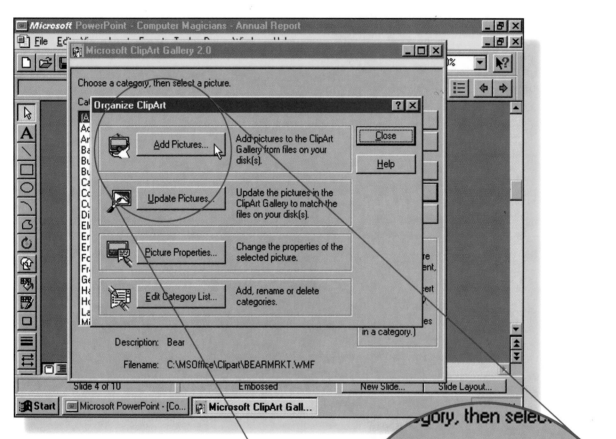

"Why would I do this?"

The Microsoft ClipArt Gallery stores all your available artwork in one central location and displays *thumbnails* (miniature pictures) of each picture so you can see what you're selecting. You can add other images to the Gallery to take advantage of those features. If you have a logo, a business card, or other artwork you're fond of in an electronic file, you can add that file to the Microsoft ClipArt Gallery.

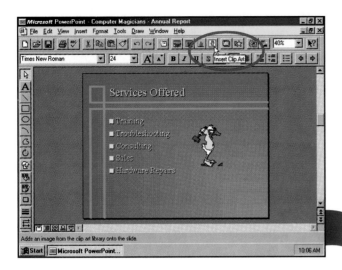

1 With any slide displayed, click the **Insert Clip Art** button. The Microsoft ClipArt Gallery dialog box appears.

2 Click the **Organize** button in the Microsoft ClipArt Gallery dialog box. PowerPoint displays the Organize ClipArt dialog box.

WHY WORRY?

If you don't like the way the ClipArt Gallery organizes graphic images, click the Edit Category List button in the Organize ClipArt dialog box to add, rename, or delete categories.

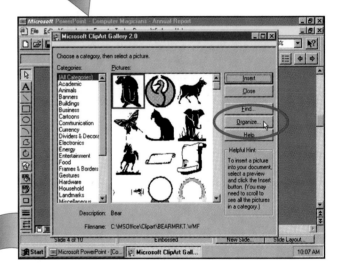

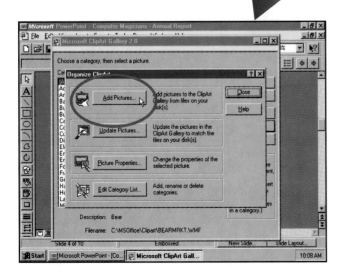

3 Click the **Add Pictures** button.

NOTE ▼

If you upgraded your current version of PowerPoint from a previous version, you might want to click the Update Pictures button. When you do, PowerPoint makes sure that your computer has all the files necessary for the thumbnails in the Gallery and discards thumbnails that are missing files.

4 Locate the graphics file you want to add to the ClipArt Gallery and click **Open**.

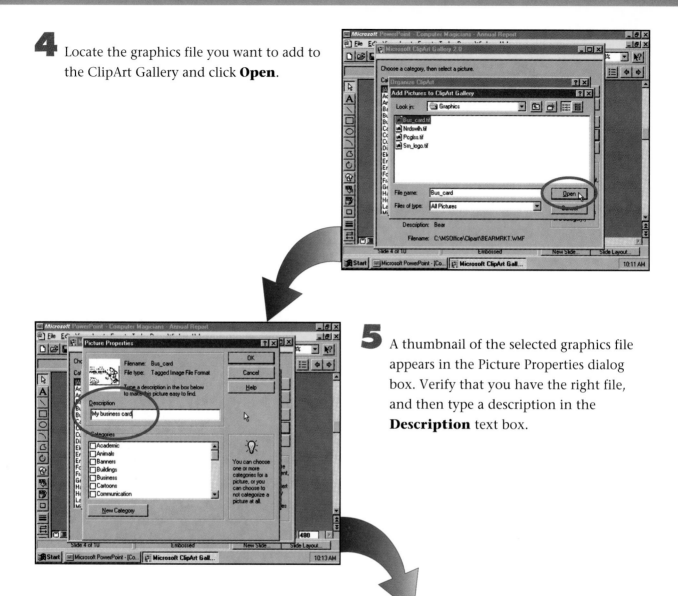

5 A thumbnail of the selected graphics file appears in the Picture Properties dialog box. Verify that you have the right file, and then type a description in the **Description** text box.

6 Click the **New Category** button to create a new ClipArt Gallery category in which to store the image. (Alternatively, you can just select one of the existing categories.)

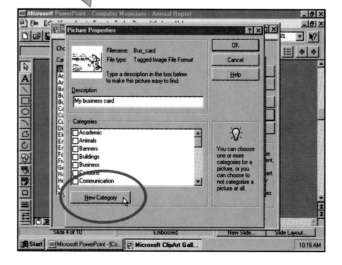

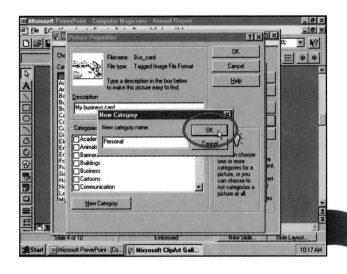

7 In the New Category dialog box, type a name for the new category and click **OK**.

8 The new category appears in the Categories list. Click on it if it isn't already selected, and then click **OK**. ■

WHY WORRY?

You can add a graphic image to more than one category, or you can choose not to assign a category at all. If you do not assign a category, the artwork appears when you select All Categories.

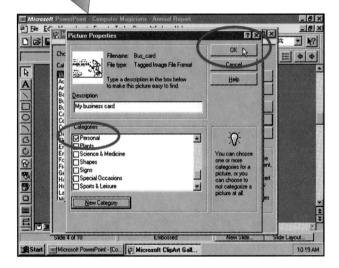

Using Drawing Tools

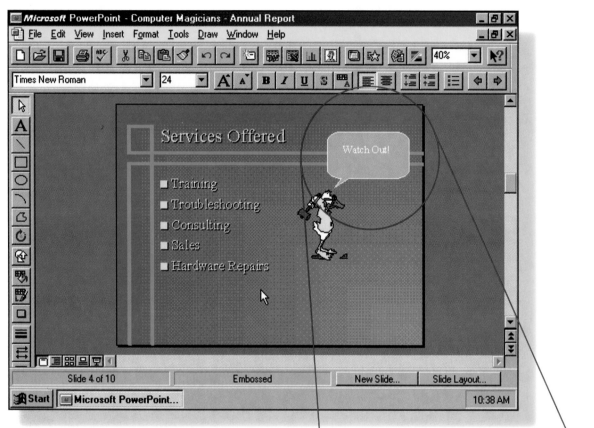

"Why would I do this?"

When you're striving to create an effective
presentation, you might want to take advantage
of special drawing tools to point out specific
features within a slide, or you might want to
add a "balloon comment" (like the bubbles that
appear above cartoon characters' heads). You
can help the audience better understand a slide
by using one of these methods.

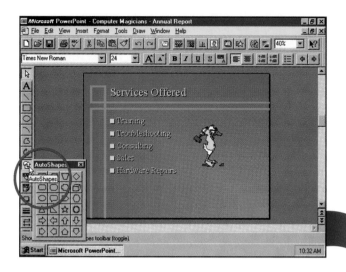

 1 Select the slide you want to draw on and click on one of the buttons on the Drawing toolbar. To add a balloon comment, for example, click on the **AutoShapes** button.

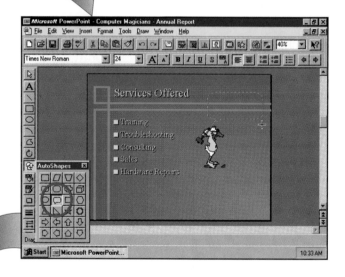

2 Click the **balloon** button. Then click and drag the shape to where you want it on the slide.

WHY WORRY?

If you don't place the shape in exactly the right spot, you can move it later.

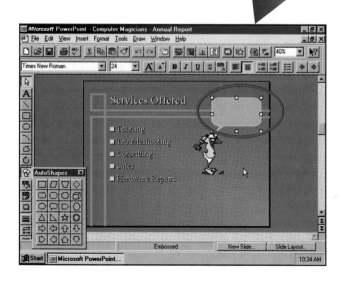

3 When the shape looks the way you want it to, release the mouse button. Handles appear around the shape, indicating that it's selected. You can move and resize this object just as you would any piece of clip art.

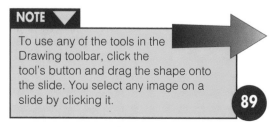

NOTE ▼

To use any of the tools in the Drawing toolbar, click the tool's button and drag the shape onto the slide. You select any image on a slide by clicking it.

89

4 To add text to the balloon, click the **Text Tool** button. Now you can give the character a voice!

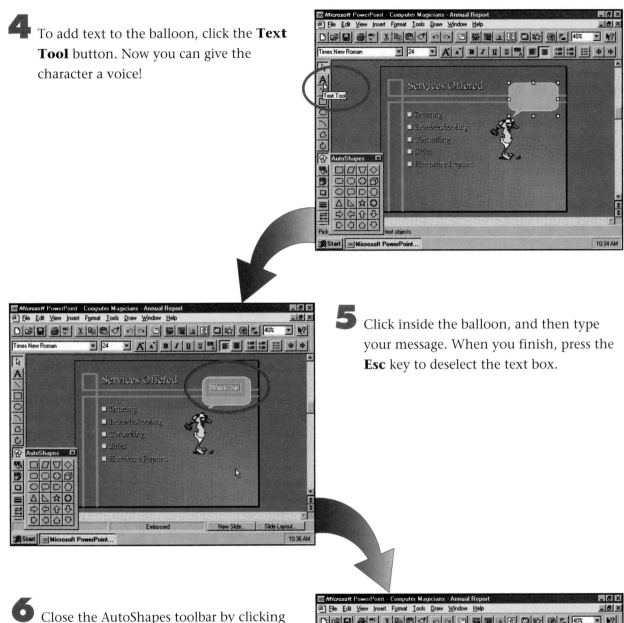

5 Click inside the balloon, and then type your message. When you finish, press the **Esc** key to deselect the text box.

6 Close the AutoShapes toolbar by clicking the **AutoShapes** button on the Drawing toolbar again. ■

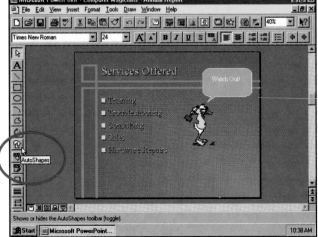

PART IV
Creating an Organization Chart

People love to look at organization charts, or *org charts*. An org chart is universally understood: it shows the specific position each person holds in a company and who each person reports to (which can be one or more persons). An org chart is an effective means of illustrating a corporate structure, and it's a natural choice for a presentation. And because corporate structures are constantly changing, it's important that you are able to easily create and modify an org chart to keep it updated.

In PowerPoint, you can insert an org chart into any slide using the Microsoft Organization Chart utility program. This program has its own menu and toolbars, and when it's open, it even has its own button on the Windows 95 taskbar. Although you open this utility from within PowerPoint, when an org chart is open, its button on the taskbar looks pushed in (which means that it is active), and the PowerPoint button does not. However, you'll still be able to see your PowerPoint presentation behind the org chart window. You can easily switch between the two programs by clicking the taskbar button for the program you want to use. Once an org chart exists on a slide, opening the Microsoft Organization Chart program is as simple as double-clicking the chart.

Buttons on the Microsoft Organization Chart toolbar enable you to easily add the different types of positions to the chart. Five types of positions can exist within an org chart: subordinate, co-worker (left), co-worker (right), manager, and assistant. These positions show *relationships between positions* and not the status of the employee within the particular organization. (So if an important person in a company reports to someone else, she should not be offended if her position is referred to as "subordinate.") You can use these five positions to build the structure of relationships that exist in any organization; in no way do they indicate status or job responsibilities.

Many tasks you'll perform on an org chart use skills you've already learned. For example, to delete a position, you select the object and press the **Delete** key; to move a position, you use drag-and-drop and move the object to a new location.

In this part of the book, you learn how to create an org chart and how to add, delete, and move people within it. You also learn how to change the style used to display a group of people so the relationships between the people are correct. You use *styles* to define relationships between clusters of workers. For example, if you have several people who report to a supervisor as a group, individually, or as members of teams, you use a particular style to define that sub-group.

When you have all the positions in your chart correctly in place, you're ready to move the chart onto the slide and resize it, if necessary. Once your org chart is on a slide, you can print it using PowerPoint's File, Print command. Because an org chart is printed as part of a slide, the Organization Chart program does not have a Print command as other programs do.

Installing Microsoft Organization Chart

Microsoft Organization Chart, the program you use to create and modify org charts, is not automatically installed when you install PowerPoint. If you attempt to create an org chart and you don't see the MS Organization Chart 2.0 option in the Object Type list (see Task 32), you'll have to install the program first.

Installing this program is easy: all you need are your original PowerPoint CD-ROM or installation diskettes and about 15 minutes. Close any open programs so that the only program that's open is Windows 95. Click the **Start** button and click **Run**. Then type **a:\setup.exe** in the **Open** text box and click **OK**. The installation program opens, knowing that you already have PowerPoint installed. Click the **Add/Remove** button and make sure the **Microsoft Organization Chart 2.0** option is checked (it's located in the Office Tools section). Then click **OK** to install the new program. The installation program lets you know when the program is installed.

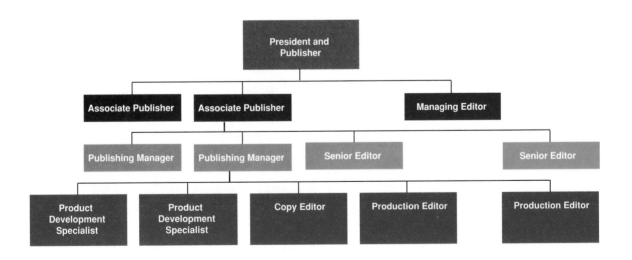

Inserting an Organization Chart on a Slide

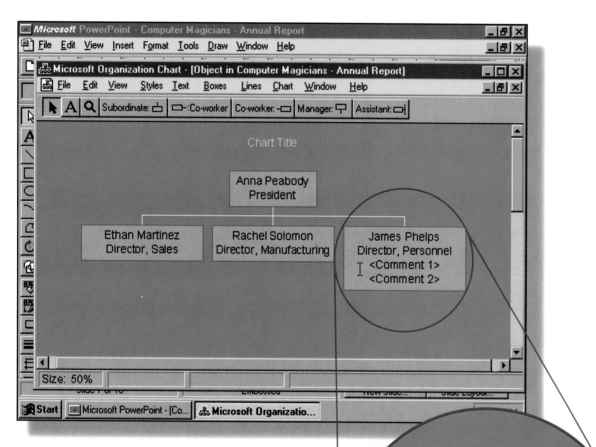

"Why would I do this?"

An organization chart (or org chart) is an attractive way of letting people know the relationships between people in a group. Sure, you could verbally describe who reports to whom, but an org chart can be far more descriptive than words and is usually easier to understand. And once you create an org chart, you can add, delete, and move people within the chart as they move within the real company.

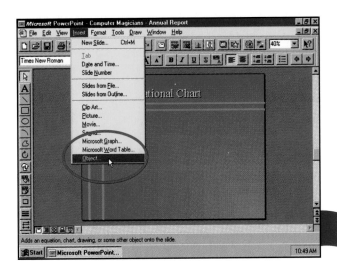

1 Make sure the slide into which you want to insert the org chart is displayed on-screen. Open the **Insert** menu and choose **Object**.

NOTE ▼

A *placeholder* marks the position where you enter a person's name and title and any optional comments.

2 The Insert Object dialog box opens on-screen. In the **Object Type** list, click on **MS Organization Chart 2.0** and click **OK**. (If this option is not in the Object Type list, you need to install the program; see the instructions at the beginning of Part IV.) PowerPoint inserts an org chart object in your slide.

NOTE ▼

An object is any image or text that has handles (white or black squares) around it when it's selected.

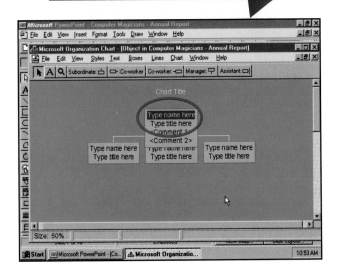

3 The Microsoft Organization Chart window opens on top of the PowerPoint window. The *placeholder* Type name here appears highlighted in the highest ranking position on the chart. Type the name you want in the selected box, and press **Enter** to add a title. If you want, you can add two lines of optional comments by pressing **Enter** after the title line.

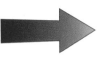

4 Click each additional placeholder that you want to replace with a name and title. Enter the appropriate information, pressing **Enter** to advance from the name to the title and comment lines.

WHY WORRY?

You don't have to replace every place-holder with text. Whether you replace a placeholder or not, only the text you do type appears in the final org chart.

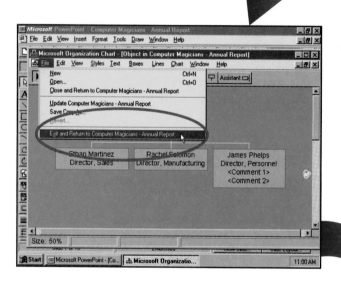

5 When you finish adding people to the org chart, you need to return to the slide. Open the **File** menu and choose **Exit and Return to** *the name of your presentation*. (The name of your presentation appears as part of the command.)

NOTE ▼

The Close and Return command is similar to the Exit and Return command. However, Close and Return automatically saves your work; Exit and Return prompts you to save your work before returning to the slide.

6 If you haven't saved your work, this dialog box appears. Click **Yes** to update the chart on the slide. (You can click No to keep the existing chart on the slide the way it is, or you can click Cancel to continue working in the Microsoft Organization Chart program.) When you return to the slide, press **Esc** to deselect the org chart. ■

NOTE ▼

You can resize and move the chart the same way you would clip art.

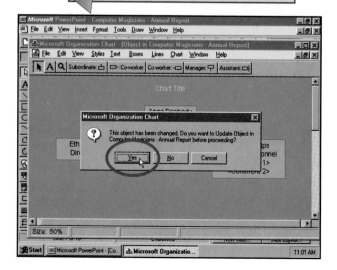

Adding a Person to an Organization Chart

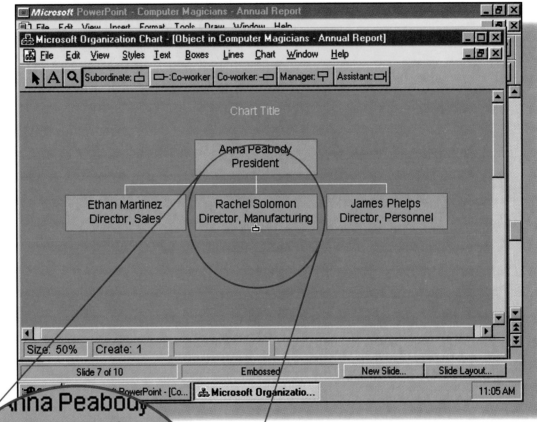

"Why would I do this?"

When a new person enters the corporate structure of your group or organization, you need to add him or her to your org chart. The Microsoft Organization Chart program makes it easy for you to add a new person to a group. When you add a person to an org chart, the Microsoft Organization Chart program automatically adds the lines to connect that person to others and adjusts the spacing and size of the placeholders.

1 Open the Microsoft Organization Chart program by double-clicking on the org chart object in the slide. Then click the toolbar button for the type of position you want to add (the **Subordinate** button, for example).

> **NOTE** ▼
>
> In most organizations, a subordinate works *for* someone, and a co-worker works *with* someone. Generally, an assistant relieves another position of responsibilities.

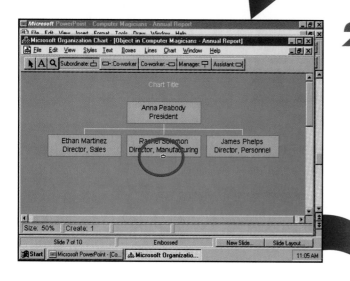

2 The mouse pointer changes to the symbol on the button you clicked. Click the placeholder for the person in relation to whom you're adding the new position. For example, if you're adding a subordinate for Rachel Solomon, you click on Rachel's position after you click the Subordinate button.

3 A placeholder appears for the new position. Type the new person's name and title and any necessary comments, pressing **Enter** to move from one to the next. ∎

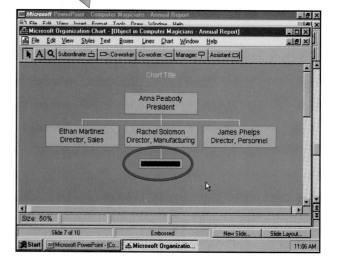

Deleting a Person from an Organization Chart

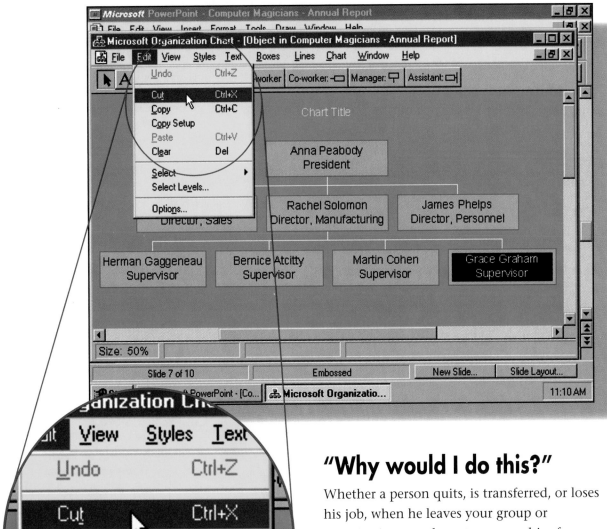

"Why would I do this?"

Whether a person quits, is transferred, or loses his job, when he leaves your group or organization, you have to remove him from your org chart. When you delete a person from an org chart, the Microsoft Organization Chart program automatically fixes the shape and appearance of the chart.

1 With the org chart open, select the position you want to delete by clicking on it.

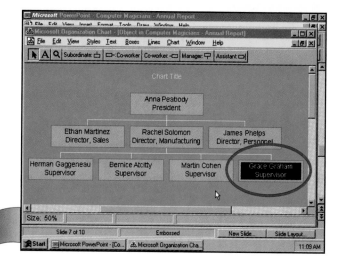

2 Open the **Edit** menu and choose **Cut**, or press the **Delete** key. Microsoft Organization Chart deletes the selected position.

WHY WORRY?

If you delete a position accidentally, choose the Edit, Undo command immediately to get it back.

3 When you delete a position, the program automatically adjusts the chart to fill in the gap. ■

TASK 35

Moving People in an Organization Chart

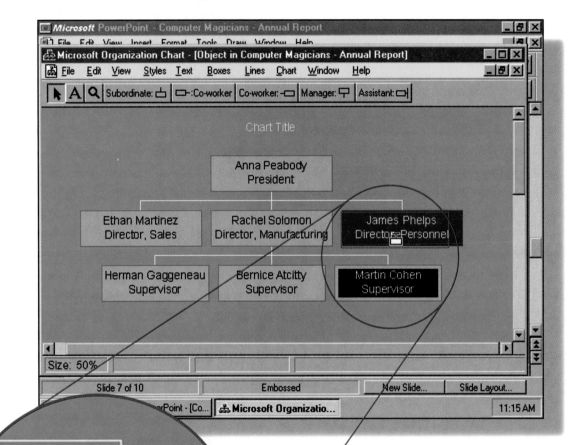

"Why would I do this?"

When your group or organization's structure changes, you need to move org chart positions from place to place or change the arrangement of groups of people accordingly. The power of an org chart program lies in its flexibility. Because people within a corporation often receive promotions or take on new responsibilities, it's important for you to be able to update your org chart easily.

103

1 With your org chart open, click on the position you want to move. Then drag it on top of the placeholder for the position to whom the selected position now reports. As you drag the position, its outline moves, and the mouse pointer takes on the shape of the position's new relationship.

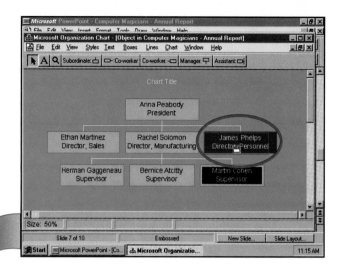

2 When the outline reaches the new location, release the mouse button. The program moves the position to its new location and adjusts the org chart as necessary.

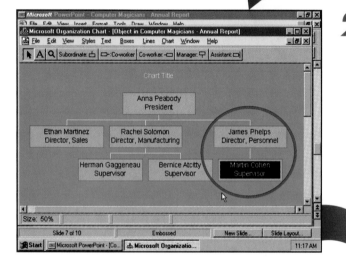

3 Press the **Esc** key to deselect the position. ■

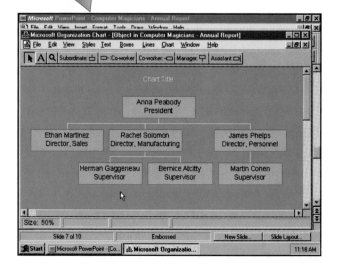

Changing Relationships Within Groups

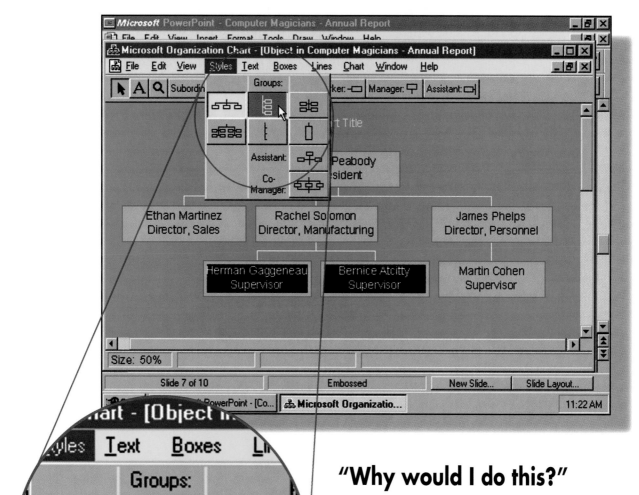

"Why would I do this?"

In most companies, the relationships between persons within departments and among groups are constantly changing and being redefined. Of course, you need to keep those relationships updated in your org chart. Microsoft Organization Chart makes it easy to change relationships between people and their positions.

1 To change the relationship between two persons in a group, double-click any member of the group. The whole group appears selected.

NOTE ▼

You can also select multiple group members by holding down the Shift key and clicking each group member.

2 Open the **Styles** menu and choose a new group style.

WHY WORRY?

If you assign a group style and then decide it isn't right, select the group and change the style again.

3 The Microsoft Organization Chart program changes the selected group to the style you selected. ■

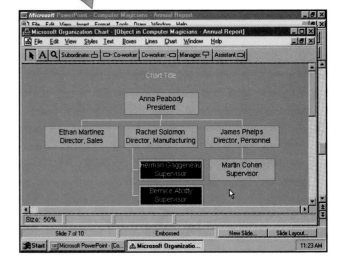

Moving an Organization Chart on a Slide

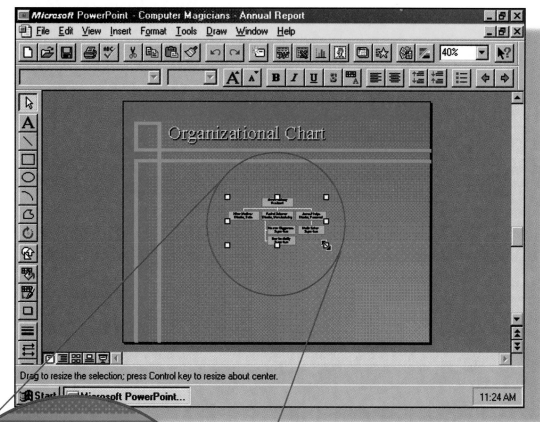

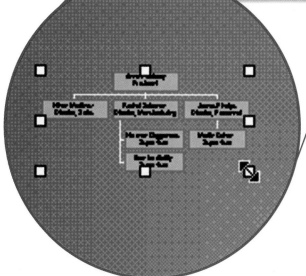

"Why would I do this?"

As you manipulate positions within an org chart, Microsoft Organization Chart makes sure that the spacing between positions looks good and that the lines connect related placeholders. When you finish with your org chart and insert it in a slide, you might want to make the chart larger or smaller or move it to a different area of the slide.

1 In Slide View, select the org chart by clicking on it. Handles (black or white squares) appear around it. Position the mouse pointer over a corner handle, and the pointer changes to a double-headed arrow.

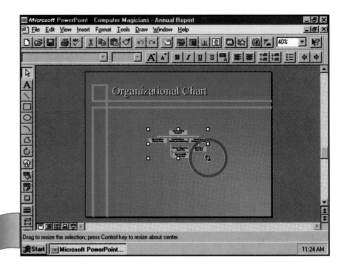

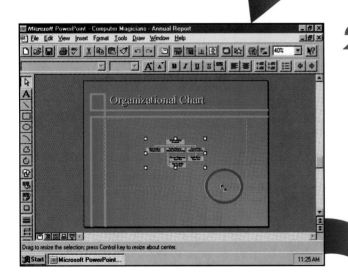

2 When you see the double-headed arrow, click on the chart and drag. An outline of the org chart moves with the mouse pointer as you drag. When the outline is the size you want, release the mouse button.

NOTE ▼

If you want your org chart to be a different size but remain in proportion, hold the Ctrl key as you drag the corner handle.

3 To move the org chart (without resizing it), click on a handle and drag until you're satisfied with the new location of its outline. Release the mouse button, and then press **Esc** to deselect the chart. ■

NOTE ▼

You may have to alternate between resizing and moving an org chart to get the shape and location exactly right.

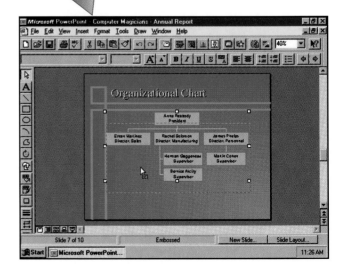

PART V

Working with Tables

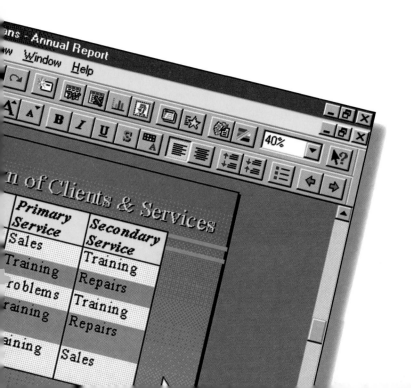

So far, you've entered text only as a title or as information on a slide. Sometimes, however, you want text or numbers in a side-by-side columnar format. Perhaps you have sales data, combinations of text and numbers that should appear side-by-side, or a list of information that would look great in several columns. This arrangement of data is called a *table*. In PowerPoint, you create a table by using a feature from another program: Microsoft Word for Windows (also called Microsoft Word or just plain Word).

A table is made up of columns and rows, and it can have headers (titles) at the top of each column. When you're working on a table, you can add or delete columns and rows, and you can change the width of a column or the height of a row. You can even make the information in a table bold, italic, or underlined just as you might any other information on a PowerPoint slide.

If you already know how to create a table in Word, you may find this part of the book boring, or you might consider it a welcome review. If you don't know how to create a table in Word, you're in for a treat! A Word table is easy to create, and just as easy to modify and make beautiful.

Because PowerPoint's table feature opens the Word program, it only works if you have Word installed on your computer. You can purchase Word individually or as part of the Microsoft Office Standard suite of programs. If you're unsure whether or not you have Word, click the **Start** button on the Windows 95 taskbar, point to **Programs**, and look for the Microsoft Word program icon. If you see the Word program icon on the menu, Word is already installed on your computer.

In this part of the book, you learn the in's and out's of working with tables. First, you create a table, and then you add information to it. Because all the data in your table isn't going to be the same size, you need to know how to change the width of your columns, which is simple with Word. And even with all the planning in the world, it's possible that you will forget information. So you'll learn how to add and delete columns and rows.

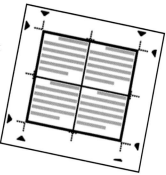

Although a table lines up the information in your slide neatly so it looks great, that's not the only reason to create one. When you use a table, you can have Word display the information in whatever order you want, such as alphabetical order from A to Z (ascending order) or alphabetical from Z to A (descending order)! Therefore, once you have all the information in your table, you'll learn how to organize and reorganize it. The process of organizing the information in a table is called *sorting*. You can sort a table by one column (last name, for example) or as many as three columns (last name, first name, and ZIP code, for example).

And finally, after you enter all your information in the table and organize it the way you want it, you can make your table attractive by adding a border to it or by using the Table AutoFormat feature to make it look like you spent hours formatting it. The AutoFormat feature contains preformatted "templates" that include colors, patterns, and character attributes (such as boldface, italics, and underlines); the templates are available in both color and black-and-white versions.

Table AutoFormat

Formats:
- List 1
- List 2
- List 3
- List 4
- List 5
- List 6
- List 7
- List 8
- 3D Effects 1
- 3D Effects 2

Preview

	Jan	Feb	Mar	Total
East	7	7	5	19
West	6	4	7	17
South	8	7	9	24
Total	21	18	21	60

OK

Cancel

Formats to Apply
- ☑ Borders
- ☑ Shading
- ☑ Font
- ☑ Color
- ☑ AutoFit

Apply Special Formats To
- ☑ Heading Rows
- ☑ First Column
- ☐ Last Row
- ☐ Last Column

Inserting a Table on a Slide

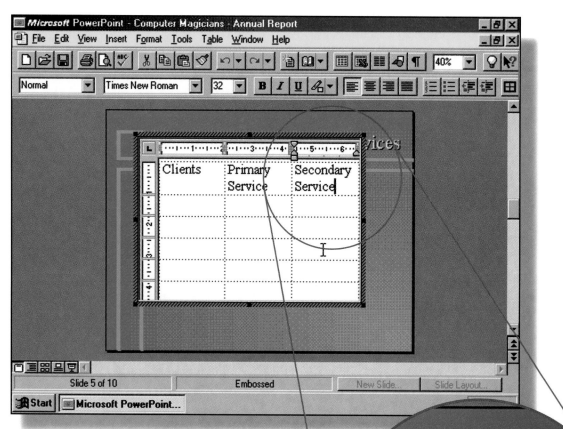

"Why would I do this?"

When you have data (text or numbers) that you
want to line up in columns, you can insert a
table on a slide. With a table, you present your
data in an easy to read and understand format.
And best of all, you don't have to type in tabs
or spaces to get the data to line up nicely.
PowerPoint enables you to create a table by
opening Microsoft Word and using its table
feature. This means you must have Microsoft
Word installed on your computer in
order to create a table.

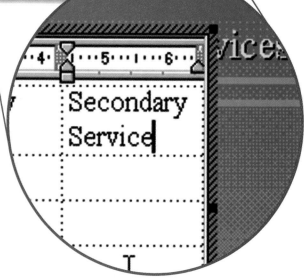

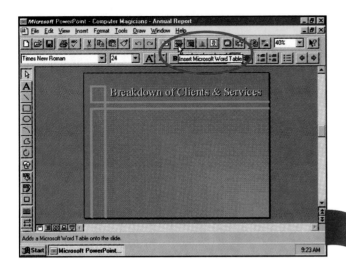

1 In Slide View, display the slide in which you want to insert the table. Then click the **Insert Microsoft Word Table** button.

WHY WORRY?

If nothing happens, or if you get an error message when you click the Insert Microsoft Word Table button, you may not have Word installed on your computer. If you know you have Word, the version you have may not be compatible with your version of PowerPoint.

2 PowerPoint displays a grid that you use to define the number of columns and rows you want in your table. Click and drag over the number of boxes you want in the table. As you drag, the dimensions appear at the bottom of the grid (number of columns × number of rows). When you're satisfied with the dimensions, release the mouse button.

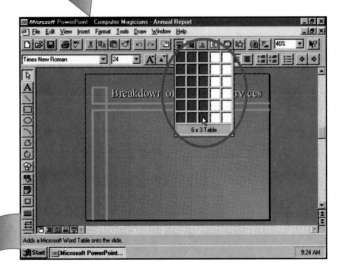

3 A table grid appears on-screen, with the number of columns and rows you specified. The *insertion point* is in the top left *cell*, or box. Enter titles for the columns, pressing **Tab** after each one to advance to the next cell.

NOTE ▼

The grid you see surrounding your table will not be visible on your slide. You learn how to add a border to your table in Task 43.

115

4 When you finish entering the column heads, click anywhere outside the table or press **Esc** to close the Word table and return to PowerPoint's Slide View. The grid disappears, but the table remains selected (as the handles indicate).

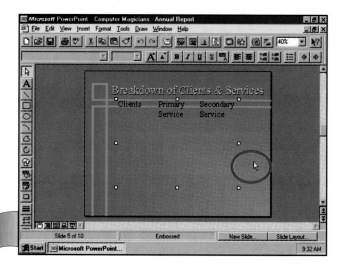

5 Click anywhere outside the table's handles or press **Esc** to deselect the table object. ∎

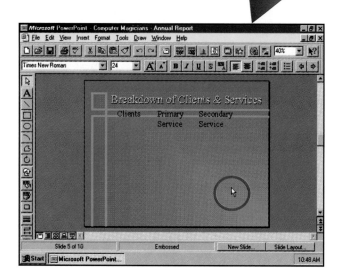

Adding Data to a Table

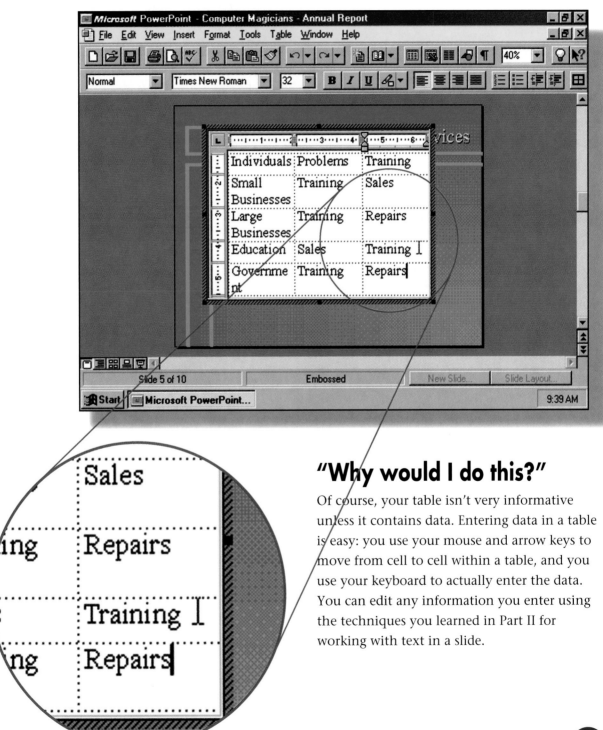

"Why would I do this?"

Of course, your table isn't very informative unless it contains data. Entering data in a table is easy: you use your mouse and arrow keys to move from cell to cell within a table, and you use your keyboard to actually enter the data. You can edit any information you enter using the techniques you learned in Part II for working with text in a slide.

117

1 Double-click the table on the slide, and the Microsoft Word program starts. Because you're using the Microsoft Word program, the toolbars and menu bar you see now are those of Microsoft Word (not PowerPoint).

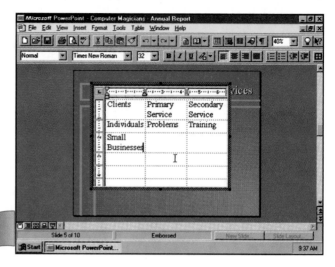

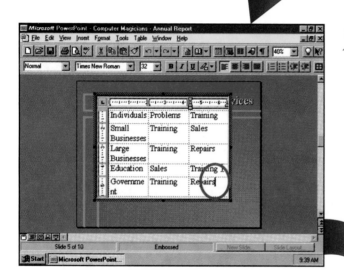

2 Move the mouse pointer to the cell in which you want to start typing. Click to position the insertion point in the cell, and then begin typing text.

WHY WORRY?

If your table doesn't have enough rows for your data, place the insertion point in the last cell of the last row and press Tab. A new row appears.

3 Press **Tab** to move the insertion point from cell to cell. If your table contains more rows than you can see, the grid scrolls as you move up or down in it. You can scroll to data that's out of sight using the keyboard's up and down arrow keys. ■

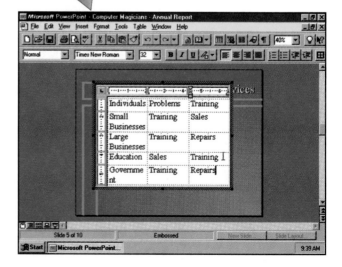

Changing Column and Row Size

"Why would I do this?"

After you enter the data, you may want to change the size of the columns in the table to make it look more attractive. If the data you enter is too wide to fit in a cell, Word wraps the leftover characters to a second line. Although it's okay to have more than one line of text in a cell, sometimes Word chops a word right in the middle. You can fix that problem by adjusting a column's width.

1 Open the Word table if necessary (see Task 38). Position the mouse pointer on the lower part of the ruler above the column whose width you want to change. The mouse pointer becomes a downward-pointing arrow.

WHY WORRY?

Sometimes it's hard to make the down arrow appear. Keep moving the mouse pointer around under the table ruler, and eventually you will find it.

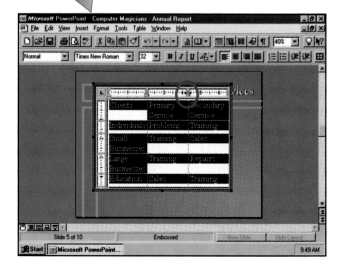

2 When the down-arrow mouse pointer appears, click and drag across all the columns in the table to select them.

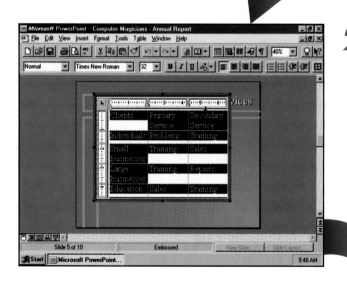

3 In the ruler, double-click in the space between two columns to indicate you want to change the column size.

NOTE ▼

When you see a double-headed horizontal arrow on the ruler, you can change the width of the selected column by dragging the mouse pointer over the existing column divider.

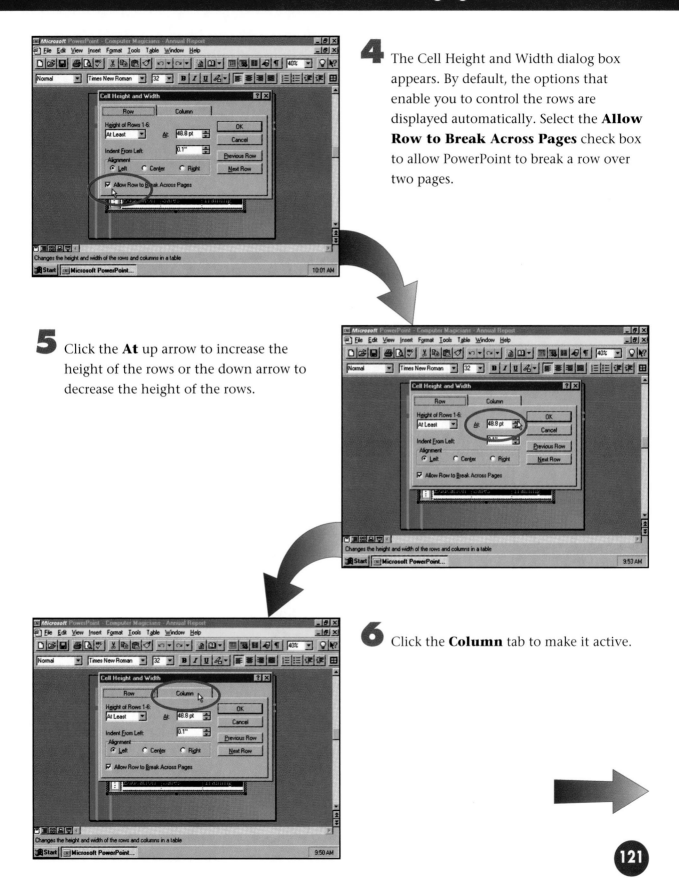

4 The Cell Height and Width dialog box appears. By default, the options that enable you to control the rows are displayed automatically. Select the **Allow Row to Break Across Pages** check box to allow PowerPoint to break a row over two pages.

5 Click the **At** up arrow to increase the height of the rows or the down arrow to decrease the height of the rows.

6 Click the **Column** tab to make it active.

7 Click the up or down arrows in the **Space Between Columns** box to increase or decrease the amount of space between columns.

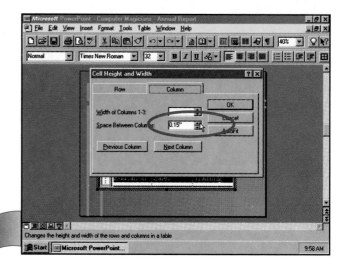

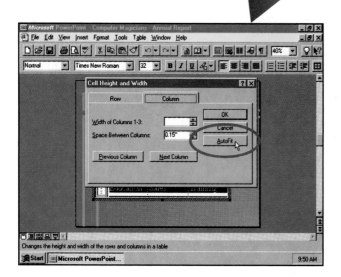

8 Click the **AutoFit** button to have Word automatically size each column to accommodate the widest text entry it contains. Click **OK**, and Word adapts the table to meet your new specifications. ■

Inserting or Deleting a Column or Row

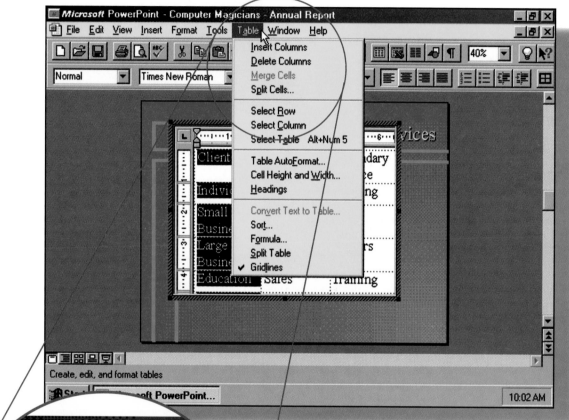

"Why would I do this?"

No matter how much time you spend planning your table, it probably won't be perfect at first. You might have to add a row for a salesperson you forgot, or you might have to delete the column for a product your company no longer carries. The Table menu makes it simple to add a column or row to a table. If you select a column first, Word gives you commands that enable you to insert or delete a column. If you select a row first, the commands enable you to insert or delete a row.

1 When you add a column, Word inserts it to the left of the selected column. Position the mouse pointer in the ruler above the column to the left of which you want to insert a new column. When the mouse pointer becomes the downward-pointing arrow, click.

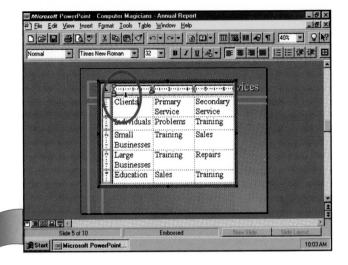

NOTE ▼

You can insert more than one column or row by selecting as many columns or rows as you want to add *before* you open the Table menu.

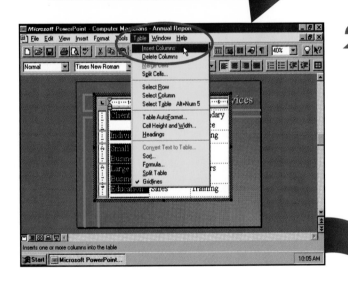

2 Open the **Table** menu. Because a column is selected, the top two commands are for working with columns. (If you had selected a row, the top two commands would mention rows.) Choose the **Insert Columns** command.

WHY WORRY?

If you don't select a column, the Table menu doesn't list the Insert Column command or the Delete Column command.

3 A new column appears to the left of the column that you selected.

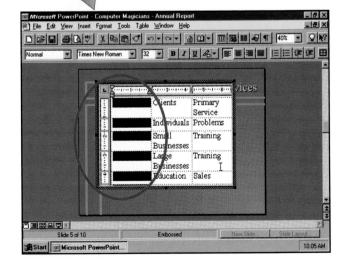

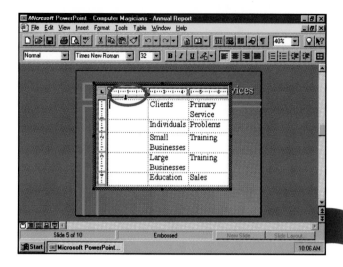

4 To delete a column, select the column using the downward-pointing arrow in the ruler. (To delete a row, select it with the horizontal arrow that appears when you place the mouse pointer on the ruler along the left side of the window.)

5 Open the **Table** menu and choose **Delete Columns**. (To delete a selected row, open the **Table** menu and choose **Delete Rows**.)

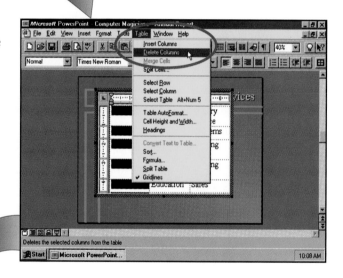

6 Word removes the selected columns (or rows) from the table. ■

Sorting Data in a Table

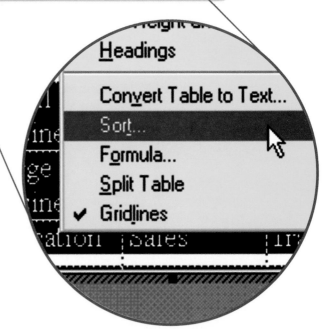

"Why would I do this?"

It's not always easy to make sure you enter your table data in the "right" order. And even if you think it's in the right order, you might have to move things around later. When you *sort* the contents of a table, Word searches a specific column or row and puts its contents in ascending or descending order. *Ascending order* arranges the elements in place from A to Z or 0 to 9; *descending order* arranges the elements in place from Z to A or 9 to 0. You can also sort data by more than one column in your table, so you can sort a list of salespersons by last name and then by first name, just like the names in a phone book.

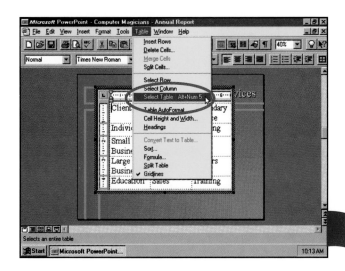

1 Open the table you want to sort, pull down the **Table** menu, and choose **Select Table**. This tells Word that you want to sort the entire table, not just part of it.

NOTE ▼

Because Word can sort your data, you can enter it in any order you want to. You don't have to waste time organizing the information; Word does it for you!

2 After you select the table, open the **Table** menu again and choose **Sort**. The Sort dialog box appears.

WHY WORRY?

If the first row in your table contains column names, select the Header Row option button; if you don't, Word sorts the column names along with your data.

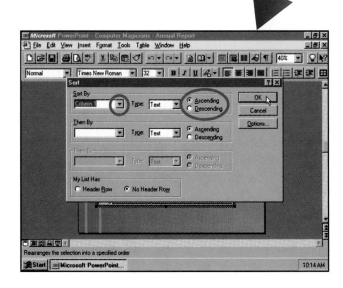

3 Click the **Sort By** drop-down list arrow and select the column you want to sort first. Then choose **Ascending** or **Descending** order. (To sort by an additional column, click the **Then By** drop-down list arrow, select the column, and select **Ascending** or **Descending** again.) When you finish entering the sort criteria, click **OK**. ■

Adding Borders and Shading to a Table

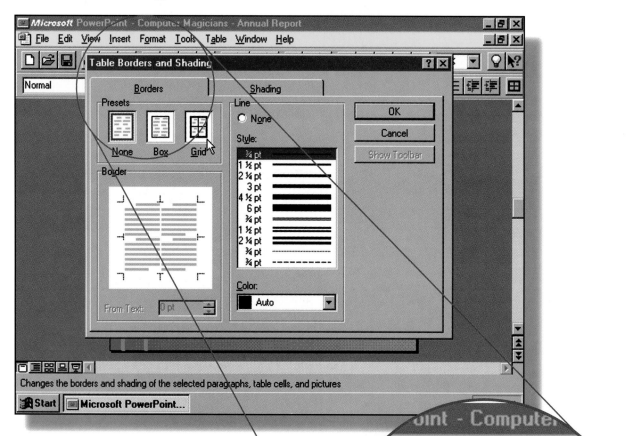

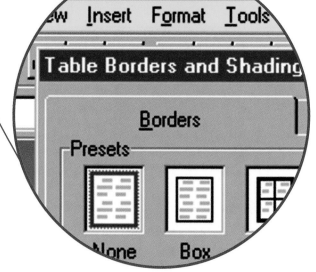

"Why would I do this?"

If you think your table looks a little "naked," you can add a border and possibly some shading! A border makes the table come alive on-screen and makes the information it contains easier to read—especially if it contains many columns and a lot of data. Shading makes it easy for the reader to follow which information is in which row or column.

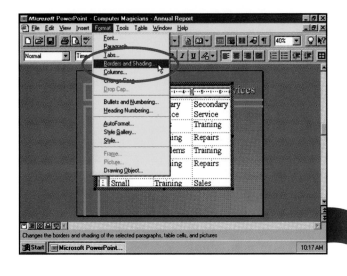

1 Open the table you want to enhance by double-clicking on it. Then open the **Format** menu and choose **Borders and Shading**. The Table Borders and Shading dialog box appears. You can add a border around the entire table or just parts of it.

2 Click on **Grid** and, if you want to, choose a new line style to make the border's lines thicker or thinner. As you make your choices, Word displays the effects of your selections in the Border box in the lower-left corner of the dialog box.

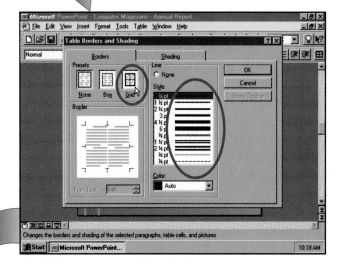

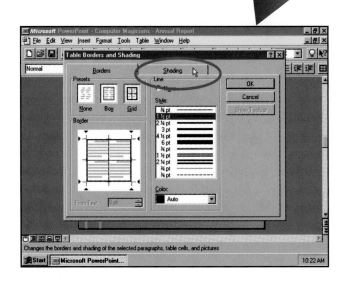

3 Click the **Shading** tab in the Table Borders and Shading dialog box to see the available shading options.

NOTE ▼

In the Presets area, None displays the table with no surrounding border and no lines between cells, Box surrounds the outside edge of the table with a border, and Grid adds a thin line between columns and rows and a thick line around the outside of the table.

4 Select the level of shading you want in your table. When you click a shading box, the **Custom** option button becomes selected.

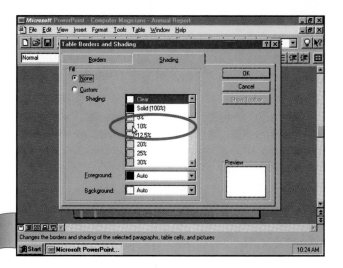

5 When you finish making your selections, click **OK**. Word displays the table with your changes in effect. ■

Using the Table AutoFormat Feature

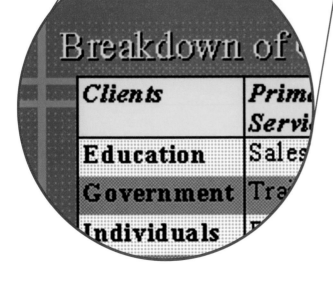

"Why would I do this?"

Although you can add borders, shading, character formatting, and so on to a table on your own, using Word's AutoFormat feature can save you a lot of time and effort. This "one-stop shopping" tool enables you to apply preformatted table styles easily. Each AutoFormat style contains fonts, attributes, colors, and borders. You can accept each AutoFormat style "as is," or you can turn certain features on or off depending on how you want your table to look.

131

1 Open the table you want to work with, open the **Table** menu, and choose **Table AutoFormat**. The Table AutoFormat dialog box appears.

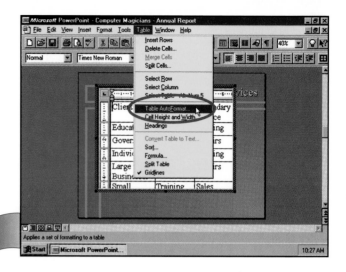

2 Word offers 32 AutoFormat styles. Click on each format, and a sample appears in the Preview box. Scroll down the list until you find one that creates the effect you want. Then select it and click **OK**.

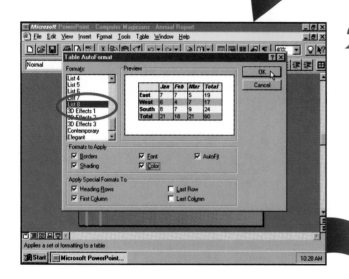

NOTE ▼

If you find a Table AutoFormat that you like but it doesn't display any colors, click the Color check box (add a check mark).

3 Word applies the Table AutoFormat you selected to the table. Press the **Esc** key twice to return to the slide and deselect the table. ■

WHY WORRY?

If you decide you want to get rid of the formatting, select the table, choose Table AutoFormat from the Table menu, and click the None option in the Table AutoFormat dialog box.

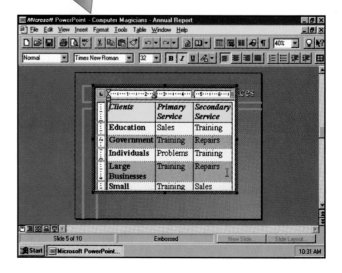

PART VI

Working with Charts and WordArt

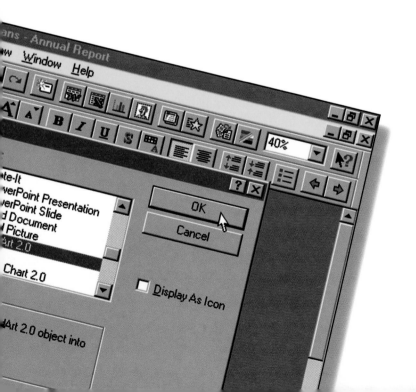

It's not always easy for the members of an audience to read the numbers in your presentations, even if a projector displays the numbers on a large screen. And in addition to being able to read the numbers, your audience has to think about what the numbers represent. It's so much easier to show the audience your numbers graphically! And in PowerPoint, transforming raw numbers into meaningful, attractive charts is simple.

In this part of the book, you'll learn how to insert a chart onto a slide and add data to it. You can add a meaningful title and modify the text within the chart by changing its font, size, and alignment. And because PowerPoint enables you to create a variety of chart types, you'll learn how to change the type of an existing chart. (Creating a chart in PowerPoint is similar to creating a chart using Microsoft Excel; if you're familiar with that program, this section will be a snap!)

The most often-used chart types are column and bar charts, which show how data changes over a period of time. You could use a column or bar chart to show your company's monthly sales during the last year. Column and bar charts have identical uses, but a column chart has vertical columns, and a bar chart has horizontal bars. The column chart is the default chart type. Another common chart type is the pie chart. You use a pie chart to display how smaller elements make up a whole entity (such as how your tax dollars are spent).

Most charts consist of an x-axis and a y-axis: the *x-axis* is the horizontal axis, and the *y-axis* is the vertical axis. You plot your data on these two axes unless you're creating a pie chart, which has no axis, or a 3-D chart, which also has a z-axis. (The *z-axis* provides depth that gives the added dimensional appearance.) All of PowerPoint's chart types are available as 2-D or 3-D charts. Whereas the 2-D charts have a flat appearance, the 3-D charts appear to have depth. A 3-D chart looks more dramatic, and you can usually rotate it to get the best view of your data.

Each group of related data in a chart (such as the twelve figures that represent monthly sales) is called a *data series*. Each individual value that's plotted (January's sales figure, for example) is called a *data point*.

Once you learn how to create a chart, you can experiment with adding special effects to text on individual slides or to all the slides in the presentation. One sure way to dazzle your audience is to use WordArt. With the WordArt feature, you can create text that looks wavy, curved, or wider at one end than at the other. You can find lots of uses for WordArt; in fact, if your company doesn't have a logo of its own, you can use WordArt to make a great one.

You learn how to insert a WordArt object on a slide and enter text into it. Then the fun begins! Enhancing WordArt means deciding what type of shape you want your text to take (there are 36 to choose from), whether to add shadow effects to the text, and what colors to use for the shadow and the text itself. (Make sure that the colors you use not only look good, but also coordinate with the colors you used on your slides.)

Fortunately, PowerPoint enables you to experiment with WordArt to find out what looks good and what doesn't—without messing up your chart. As you try different looks, the WordArt window shows you instantly what your finished WordArt looks like, so there's never a mystery. You can keep playing with it until you find the look that's right for your presentation.

Your final WordArt image is an object that you can use like any piece of clip art. Because WordArt is an object, you can change its size or move it to a new position. If you place your WordArt creation on the Slide Master, it appears on all the slides in the presentation—whether there's one slide or 1,000. Imagine the time WordArt can save you!

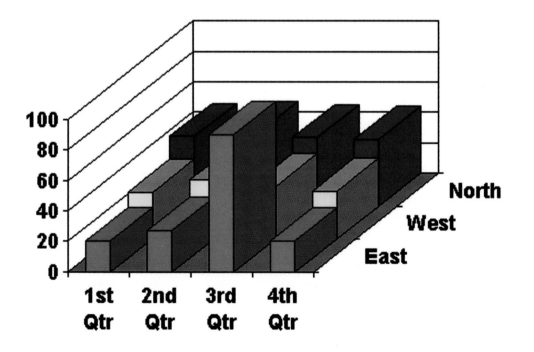

Inserting a Chart on a Slide

"Why would I do this?"

A chart presents data in a graphical format so that people are better able to see trends in data and pick up on the point you are making. By turning numeric data into a chart, you can make the data (and your audience) come alive. And when you use a chart on a slide, you don't have to worry about your numbers being small and illegible—as they often are in traditional (boring) presentations.

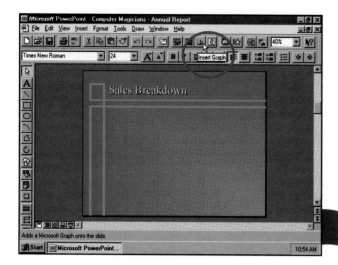

1 In Slide View, open the slide on which you want to insert a chart. Click the **Insert Graph** button. PowerPoint opens the Microsoft Graph program, which you use to enter your chart data and create the chart.

NOTE ▼

The terms *chart* and *graph* are interchangeable.

2 The Microsoft Graph datasheet grid opens. The data in this grid is default data (placeholders). To delete the default data, click in the cell in the upper-left corner and drag to cell D3. Click the **Cut** button to get rid of the data in the selected cells.

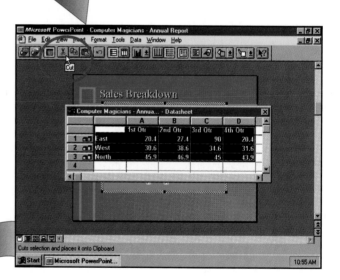

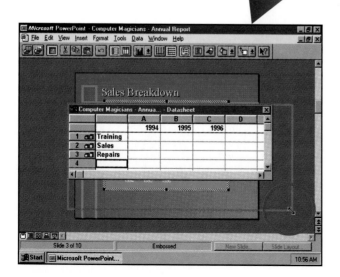

3 To make the datasheet larger so you can see more of your work, position the mouse pointer over the lower-right corner, press and hold the left mouse button, and drag. When the outline reaches the desired size, release the mouse button.

4 Click in a cell and type the information you want there. If you're typing data in columns, press **Enter** to move to the cell below the current cell. You can also click in any cell or use the arrow keys to move to it. (When you press an arrow key, the cursor moves once in that direction.)

NOTE ▼

While you're in a cell, you can use the Backspace and Delete keys to erase any mistakes you make.

5 When you finish entering your data and you're ready to see a chart, click the **View Datasheet** button. View Datasheet is a *toggle* button. When it's enabled (it appears to be pushed in), you see the datasheet grid. When it's not enabled, you see the chart.

WHY WORRY?

If the titles on the x-axis don't look good, turn to Task 47 to learn how to modify them.

6 Click the **By Column** button to change the way the data appears in the chart. You can change from By Row to By Column and vice versa. The difference between charting by column and by row is the way in which the data is arranged within the chart: when you switch the view, the data on the x-axis and the legend change places. Press the **Esc** key twice to return to the slide and deselect the chart. ∎

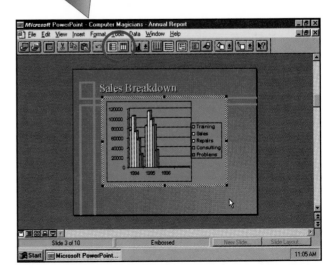

TASK 46
Adding Chart Data

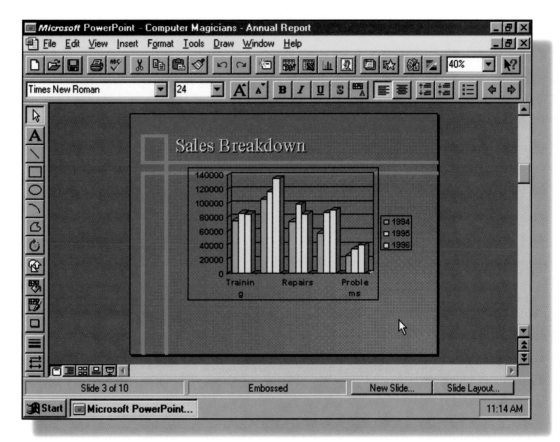

"Why would I do this?"

When you create a chart, you make a lot of decisions about how you want to display your data. Yet after you finish a chart, you may find that you need to add more data (maybe you left out a player in your softball team's stats chart, or you were just given another sales territory and need to add it to your chart). Adding data to a chart is easy. You can switch back and forth between the datasheet and the chart, adding data to the datasheet and checking out the instant results in the chart.

1 Open the chart by double-clicking it on the slide. The Microsoft Graph toolbar appears, and a thatched border surrounds the chart. Click the **View Datasheet** button to switch back to the datasheet grid, in which you enter additional data.

NOTE ▼

Microsoft Graph automatically determines the scale the y-axis uses.

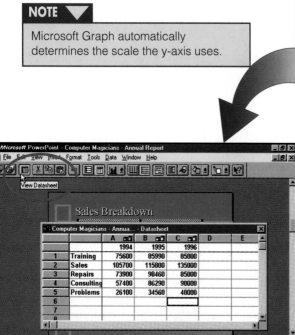

2 Click the empty cells in the next available column and type your data. When you finish, click the **View Datasheet** button to switch back to the chart and see the results of your additions.

3 To make your chart wider, position the mouse pointer over a handle. The mouse pointer turns into a double-headed arrow. Click and drag the double-headed arrow until the size of the outline satisfies you. Then release the mouse button. ■

WHY WORRY?

If you don't like the column chart (which is the default style), choose another chart style, as explained in Task 49.

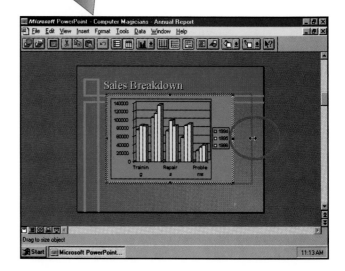

Modifying Chart Text

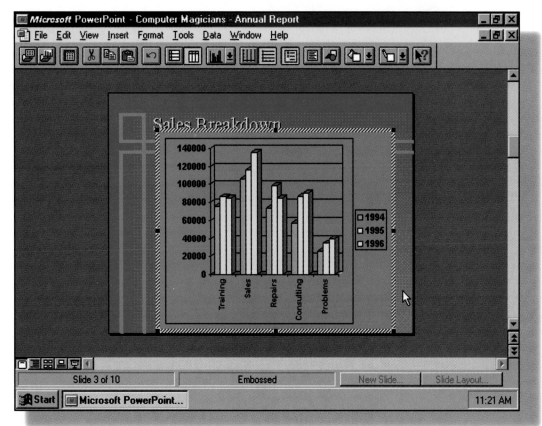

"Why would I do this?"

Microsoft Graph does a terrific job of creating a chart, but sometimes the text in the chart doesn't look quite the way you want it to. For example, the point size of column text may be too large for the number of columns in your chart. No problem! You can modify the fonts in the chart and their sizes. You can also change the alignment of the text from horizontal to vertical.

1 Double-click the chart to open it, and then click on any text you want to modify. Microsoft Graph displays handles at either end of the axis the text is on.

WHY WORRY?

It can be hard to find handles on an axis. Keep looking, though, because the handles are there!

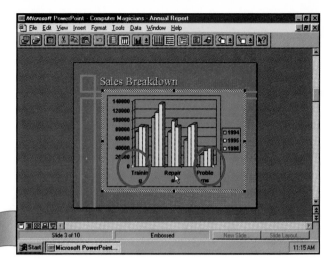

2 Open the **Format** menu and choose **Font**. The Format Axis dialog box appears.

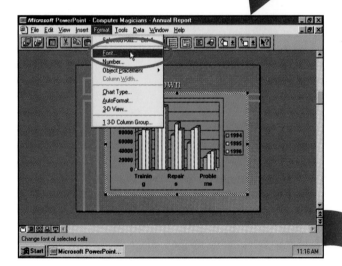

3 Click the **Font** tab if it's not selected. The Font tab lists all the fonts installed on your computer. Make the selections you want, changing the font, style, and size for the chart text.

NOTE ▼

Too many fonts can detract from your chart. Try to limit the number of fonts you use to two.

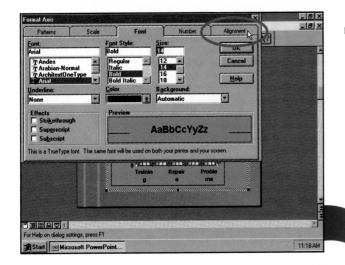

4 To change the alignment of the column text, click the **Alignment** tab.

5 In the **Orientation** box, click the sample of the alignment you want to use. Click **OK**.

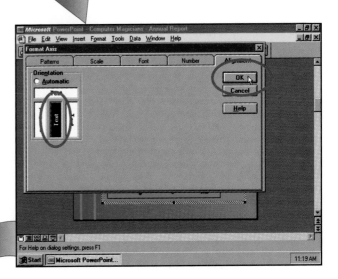

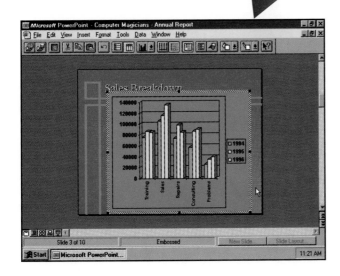

6 Microsoft Graph returns you to the chart so you can see the changes. ◼

WHY WORRY?

If you don't like the changes you made, you can return to the Format Axis dialog box and modify the text as many times as necessary until you get everything just the way you want it.

Adding a Chart Title

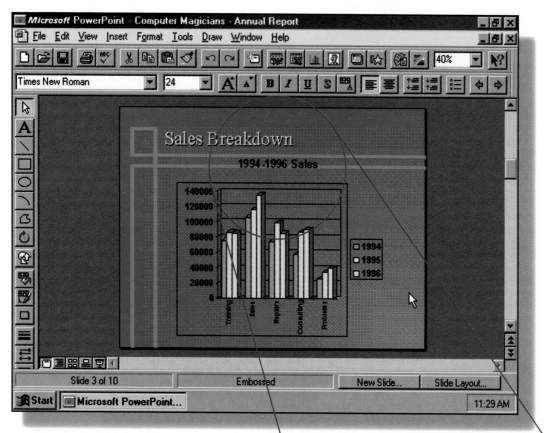

"Why would I do this?"

Even if you already have a title on your slide, you may want to include a chart title as additional information. Microsoft Graph makes it simple to add such text to your slide. Like other text in the slide, the title is preformatted, so you don't have to adjust its font, size, or location—but you can if you want.

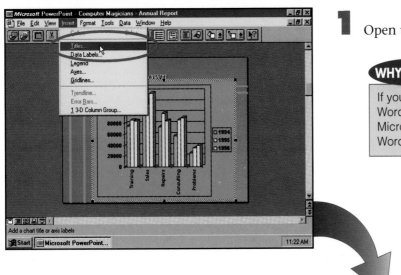

1 Open the **Insert** menu and choose **Titles**.

WHY WORRY?

If you've created charts in Microsoft Word, you already know how to use Microsoft Graph. It's the same program Word uses to create charts.

2 Click the **Chart Title** check box and click **OK**. You can also add titles to the x-axis and z-axis by clicking the appropriate check boxes.

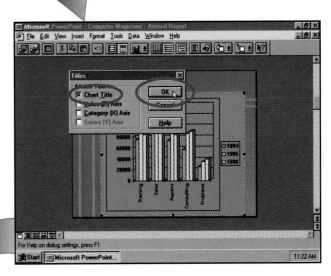

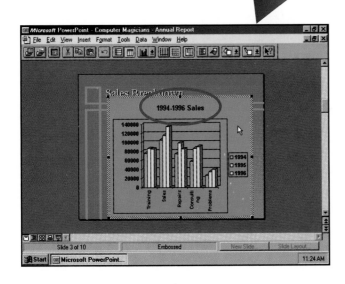

3 In the text box that appears, type the text you want to enter as the title. Then click anywhere within the chart.

NOTE

You can move the title by clicking within the text box and dragging the object to a new location.

147

4 To make room for the new title, Power-Point might have to reduce your chart size. You can resize the chart by positioning the mouse pointer over a handle until it becomes a double-headed arrow. Drag the double-headed arrow pointer until you're happy with the outline size, and then release the mouse button.

NOTE ▼

To make sure your text fits on an axis, use short words for the column and row titles.

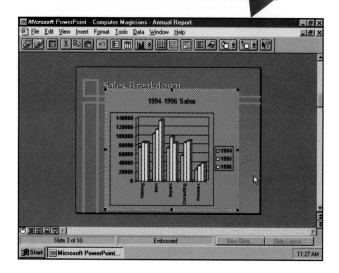

5 Microsoft Graph adjusts the chart to accommodate your title and the size changes. Press **Esc** to deselect the chart. ■

WHY WORRY?

If your text still doesn't fit the way you want it to, keep adjusting font sizes and the chart's dimensions until everything fits.

Changing the Chart Type

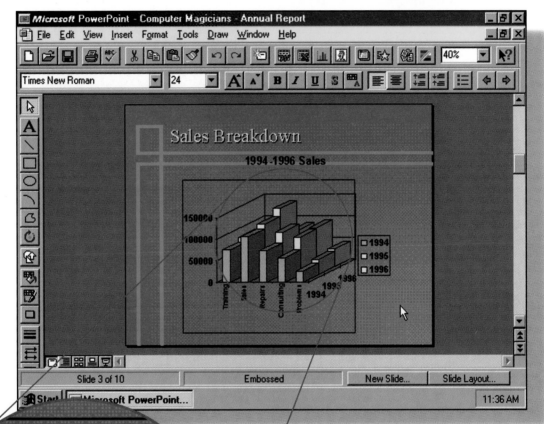

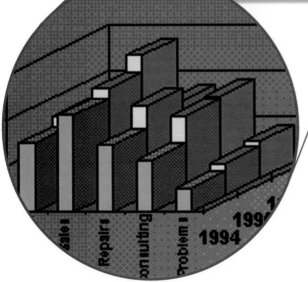

"Why would I do this?"

Microsoft Graph offers a wide variety of chart types. When you first create a chart, Microsoft Graph uses the column chart type by default. However, the program enables you to change the chart to whatever type you want. For example, you may want to use a different type of chart to show off your data better, or you may want to show your data in two different ways.

1 Double-click the chart to open Microsoft Graph. Click the **Chart Type** drop-down list arrow on the Microsoft Graph toolbar.

> **NOTE** ▼
>
> The Chart Type button shows the current chart type next to the down arrow.

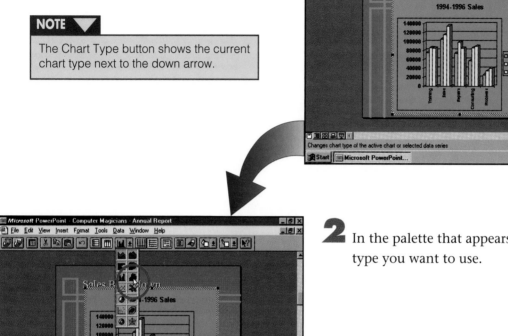

2 In the palette that appears, click the chart type you want to use.

3 Microsoft Graph applies the new chart type to your data and displays it in the chart window. 3-D chart types enable you to manipulate the chart by rotating the data. This comes in handy because you can hide columns of data in certain charts (if their data is irrelevant in a particular situation, for example) when you change chart types.

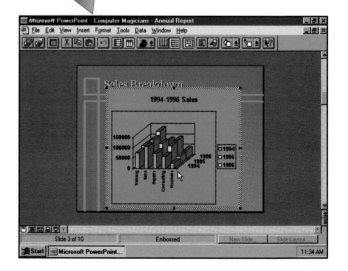

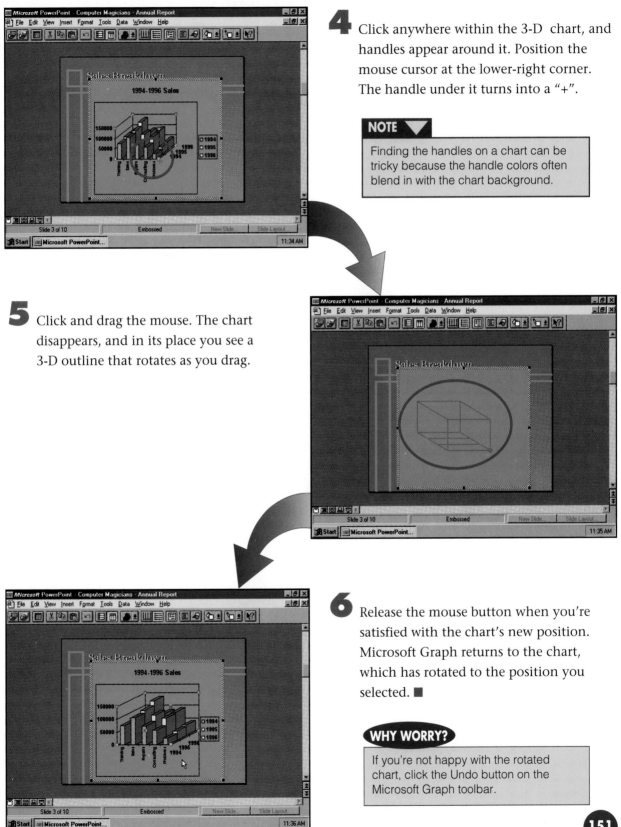

4 Click anywhere within the 3-D chart, and handles appear around it. Position the mouse cursor at the lower-right corner. The handle under it turns into a "+".

NOTE ▼

Finding the handles on a chart can be tricky because the handle colors often blend in with the chart background.

5 Click and drag the mouse. The chart disappears, and in its place you see a 3-D outline that rotates as you drag.

6 Release the mouse button when you're satisfied with the chart's new position. Microsoft Graph returns to the chart, which has rotated to the position you selected. ■

WHY WORRY?

If you're not happy with the rotated chart, click the Undo button on the Microsoft Graph toolbar.

Inserting a WordArt Object

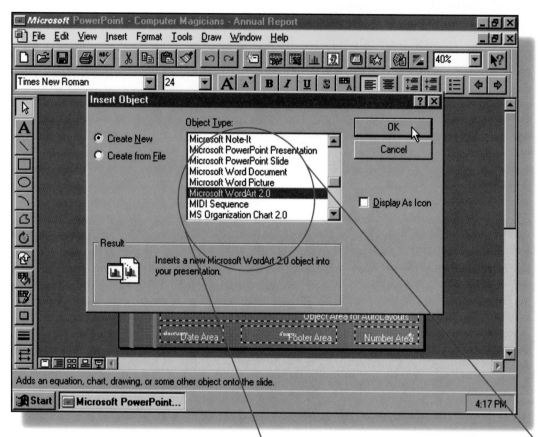

"Why would I do this?"

Have you ever seen text that looks like it's stretched or bent around a curve? You can create these effects in your slides with a feature called WordArt. WordArt offers 25 shapes and enables you to change the shading and colors of the text. You can choose to add a WordArt object to an individual slide, or you can insert WordArt on the Slide Master so it appears on every slide in your presentation.

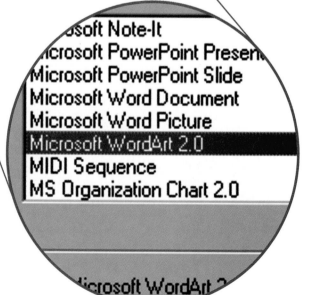

152

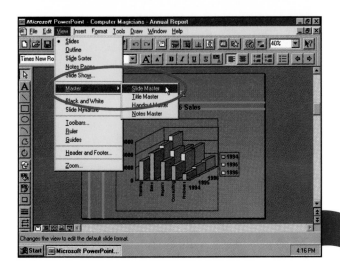

1 To open the Slide Master from any view, open the **View** menu, choose **Master**, and choose **Slide Master**.

NOTE ▼

You can also open the Slide Master by holding down the Shift key and clicking the Slide View button.

2 With the Slide Master open, open the **Insert** menu and choose **Object**.

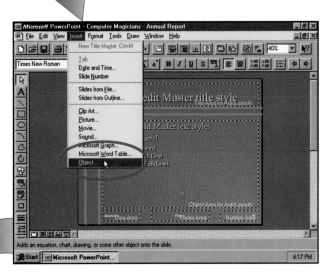

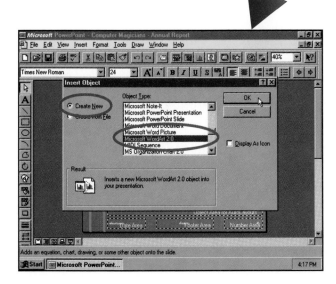

3 Select the **Create New** button if necessary. Then scroll down the **Object Type** list, click **Microsoft WordArt 2.0**, and click **OK**.

WHY WORRY?

If you don't see the Object Type list, click the Create New button. When it's selected, the Object Type list appears.

4 Type your WordArt text in the Enter Your Text Here dialog box and click **Update Display**. WordArt replaces the Your Text Here placeholder in the WordArt window with your new text.

5 To add a special shape to your text, click the **Text Shape** drop-down list arrow (at the left end of the WordArt toolbar) and select the shape you want to apply.

6 Your text takes on the shape you selected, and the shape appears in the Text Shape list box.

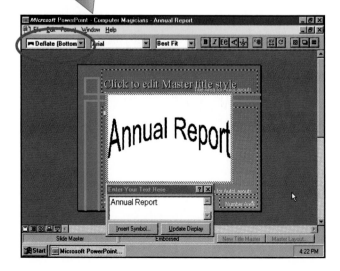

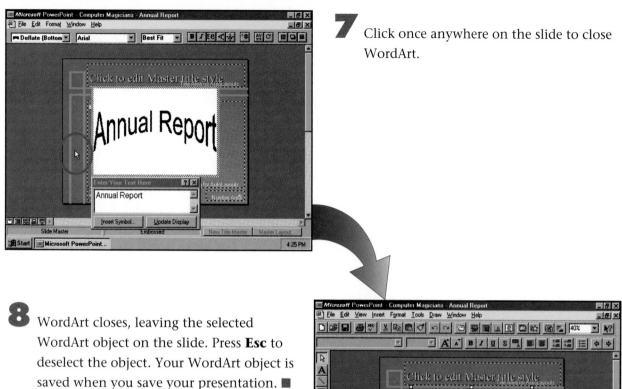

7 Click once anywhere on the slide to close WordArt.

8 WordArt closes, leaving the selected WordArt object on the slide. Press **Esc** to deselect the object. Your WordArt object is saved when you save your presentation. ■

Enhancing WordArt

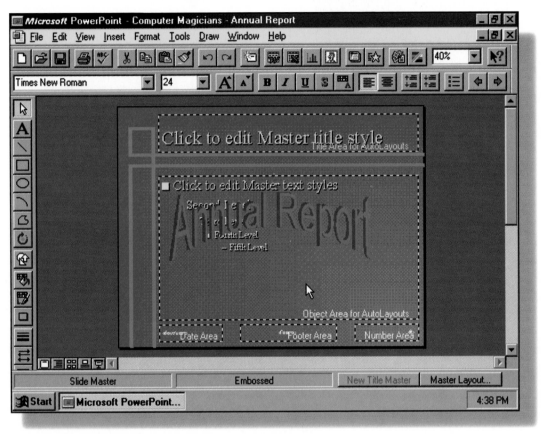

"Why would I do this?"

If you think your WordArt object looks cool
now, just wait! You can add shadows and colors
to your WordArt so that it looks really wild.
People will think you spent hours working on
this! Adding a shadow to your text gives it
depth as well as a "rich" quality, which makes
WordArt an ideal candidate for creating a
corporate logo.

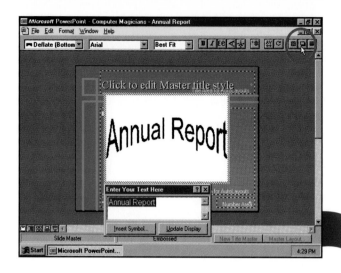

1 Double-click the WordArt object to open WordArt. Click the **Shadow** button on the WordArt toolbar.

2 In the Shadow dialog box, click the button for the type of shadow you want to apply. Each of these shadows shows the effect of light coming from a different angle, and one reverses the effect with white text on a black background.

WHY WORRY?

Make sure the colors you choose go well with the colors in your slide's background. You may have to do a little experimenting to find out which colors work as shadows and which don't.

3 To change the color of the shadow, click the **Shadow Color** drop-down list arrow and select the color you want. Click **OK** when you're satisfied with your choices.

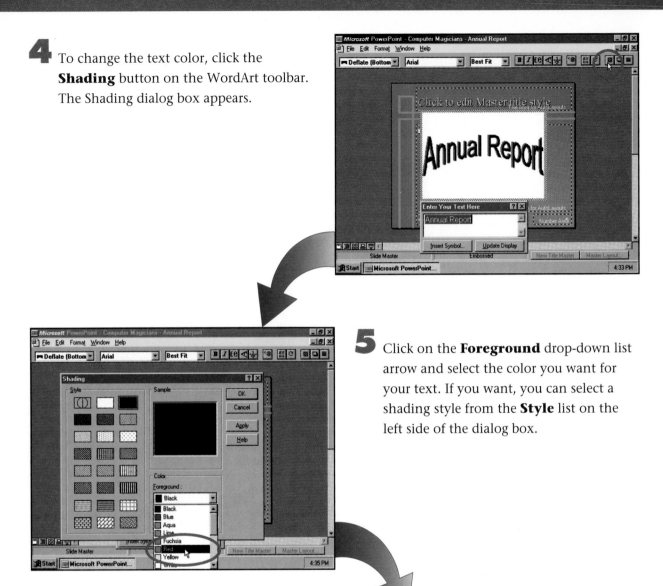

4 To change the text color, click the **Shading** button on the WordArt toolbar. The Shading dialog box appears.

5 Click on the **Foreground** drop-down list arrow and select the color you want for your text. If you want, you can select a shading style from the **Style** list on the left side of the dialog box.

6 When you're satisfied with your choices, click **OK**. Click anywhere on the slide to close WordArt, and then press **Esc** to deselect the WordArt object. ■

Sizing and Moving WordArt

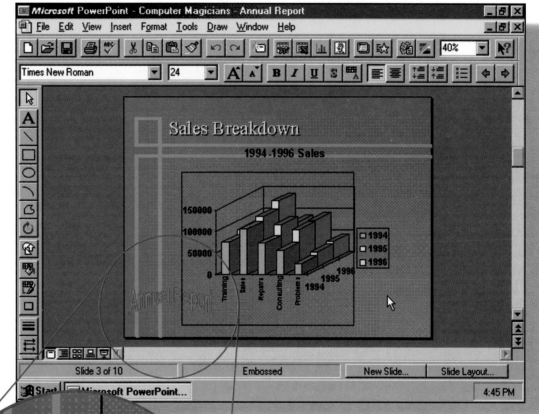

"Why would I do this?"

When you finish creating your WordArt, it appears in the center of your screen—and is probably much too large for your purposes. You can resize and move the WordArt just as you would move and resize clip art. You'll think of lots of uses for WordArt now that you know that you can control its size and location.

1 Click on your WordArt object to select it. Handles appear around it.

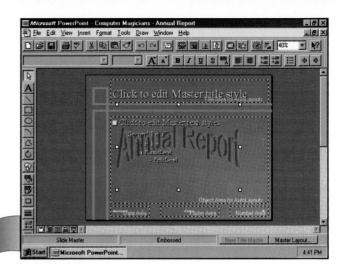

2 Position the mouse pointer over the lower-right handle until it turns into a double-headed arrow.

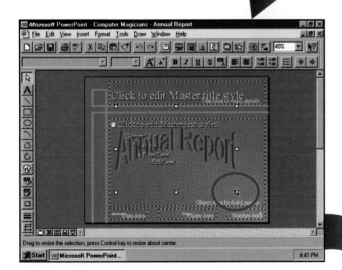

3 Press and hold the **Ctrl** key and drag the double-headed arrow pointer to make the WordArt smaller while maintaining its proportions. When the outline reaches the size you want, release the mouse button.

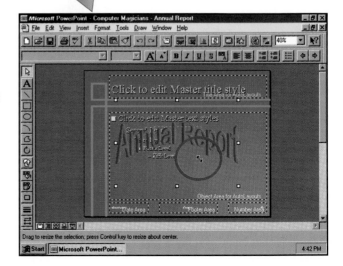

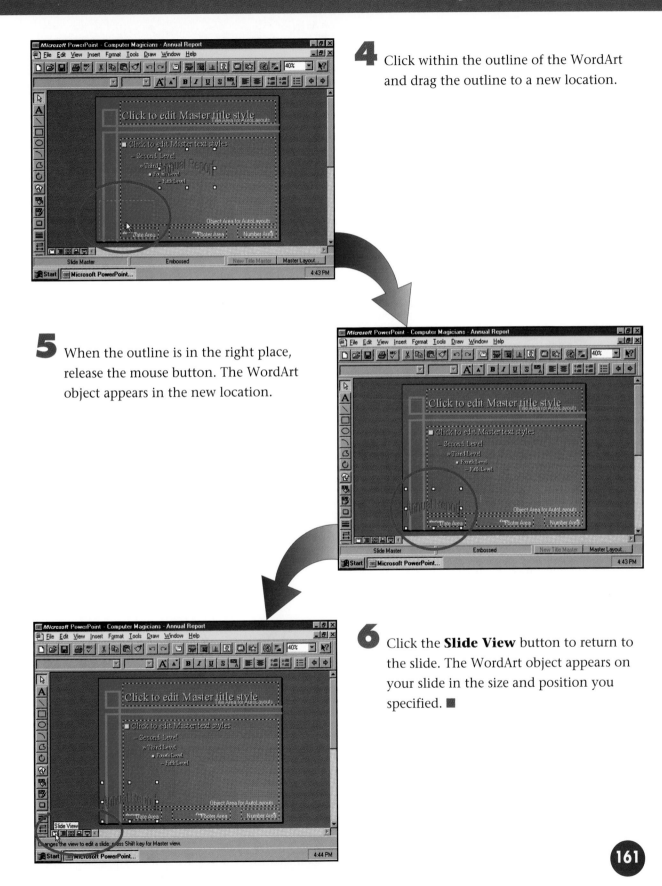

4 Click within the outline of the WordArt and drag the outline to a new location.

5 When the outline is in the right place, release the mouse button. The WordArt object appears in the new location.

6 Click the **Slide View** button to return to the slide. The WordArt object appears on your slide in the size and position you specified. ■

PART VII

Working in Outline View

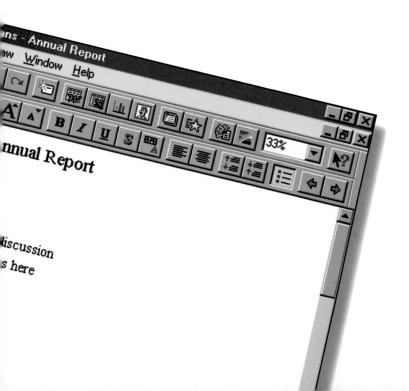

So far, you've worked exclusively in the graphical world of slides. You've created and edited individual slides and added text, colors, patterns, artwork, tables, and charts. While you were working on each slide, you knew exactly how that slide would look.

Sometimes, however, you don't need to see every graphical aspect of a slide. In fact, sometimes the graphics on a slide can distract you from analyzing the textual content of your slides. It's those times that you need Outline view.

PowerPoint's Outline view enables you to view your slides in a text-only format so you can analyze your text without having the distractions of slide backgrounds and graphic images. Next to each line of text on a slide, PowerPoint displays either a slide number and icon (if it's the slide title) or a bullet. Although no graphic images appear, you can still tell if a slide contains graphics by the appearance of the slide's icon (which appears next to the slide title). A slide having contents other than text has an icon with a small graphic image on it, while a slide containing only text has a blank icon. In addition, Outline view has its own toolbar that enables you to move text up and down within the presentation. (You can also use the drag-and-drop techniques to move text within an outline.)

Whereas in Slide view you can display only one slide on the screen at a time, in Outline view, you can see the text from as many as a dozen slides at once—depending on how large your monitor is, of course. On the other hand, if you don't want to see every line of text on each slide, you can condense each slide's information so that only the title is visible. You can condense slide details for individual slides or for all the slides in a presentation. An underline appears under the slide's title when you compress the slide's details.

You edit slide text in Outline view in much the same way you edit text in Slide view. After you select the text, you can delete or replace it using regular mouse or keyboard editing techniques. If you add, edit, or move text in Outline View, those changes appear on your slides when you switch to any other view. And although you won't see any graphic images on your slides, you will see text formatting (such as boldface, italics, and underlining) unless you choose to turn the formatting off.

Outline view makes it easy to rearrange things in your presentation. You can use drag-and-drop or the buttons on the Outline toolbar to change the order of the slides. The real advantage of Outline view, however, is that it enables you to move text. Either by using drag-and-drop techniques or by using the buttons on the Outline toolbar, you can change the position of text—whether the text is a bulleted item or a slide title. The following table shows the Outline toolbar buttons.

Outline Toolbar Buttons

Button	Name	Description
⬅	Promote (Indent less)	Makes a text line more important by decreasing the amount of indention.
➡	Demote (Indent more)	Makes a text line less important by increasing the amount of indention.
⬆	Move Up	Moves a text line up one position.
⬇	Move Down	Moves a text line down one position.
▬	Collapse Selection	Hides the details in the selected slide so that only the slide title appears.
✚	Expand Selection	Displays the details in the selected slide so that all the slide contents appear.
⬆☰	Show Titles	Hides the details of all the slides in a presentation.
⬇☰	Show All	Displays the details of all the slides in a presentation.
A̲A̲	Show Formatting	Hides/Displays the formatting used in slides.

In this part, you learn to use Outline view to organize your presentation so that the slides and the text within each slide progress logically.

TASK 53

Selecting a Slide in Outline View

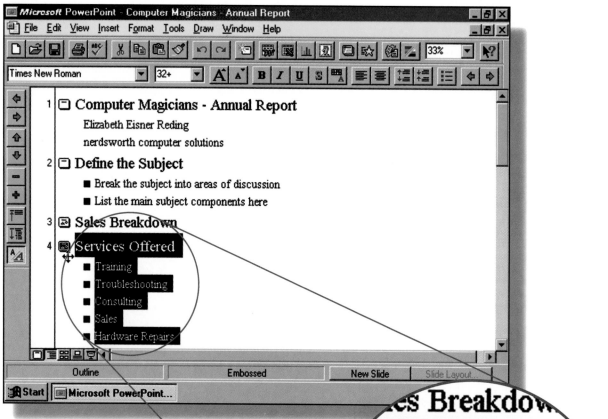

"Why would I do this?"

When you want to focus on the text in your slides without seeing the design backgrounds and individual graphic images, you use Outline view. The Outline view provides a simple, uncluttered work area in which you can edit text within slides and change the order of the text and slides. Before you can work with a slide's text, you must select the slide.

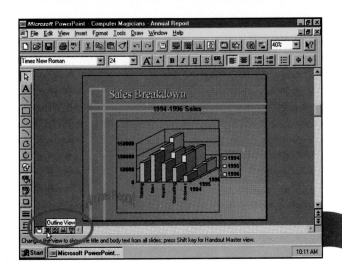

1 From any PowerPoint view, click the **Outline View** button.

NOTE ▼

Although the Standard and Formatting toolbars remain visible, Outline view displays its own toolbar along the left side of the window. The tools on the Outline toolbar enable you to move, hide, and display the text on your slides.

2 When you position the mouse pointer near a slide icon, the pointer changes to a four-headed arrow. With the four-headed arrow pointer, click on the slide icon you want to select.

WHY WORRY?

You never lose your place when you switch to Outline view because the active slide in the previous view is also active in the new view.

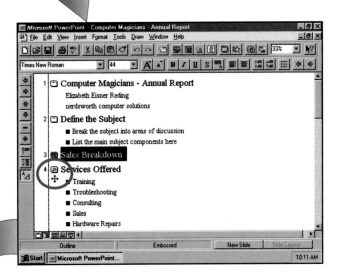

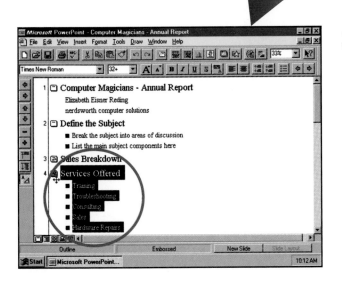

3 When you select a slide, the entire slide—including all the detail text—appears highlighted. ■

NOTE ▼

If the icon to the right of the slide number is empty, the slide does not contain graphics; if the icon has shapes on it, the slide does contain graphic images.

Hiding and Displaying Data

"Why would I do this?"

When you work in the Outline view, you may
want to see the "big-picture" of the outline so
you can make any necessary organizational
changes. To do that, you hide the details of
your slides and view only the titles. When you
finish looking at the big picture, you simply tell
PowerPoint to display the details again. You can
hide and display details on one or more selected slides (as explained in steps 1–3) or in all
the slides (as explained in steps 4 and 5).

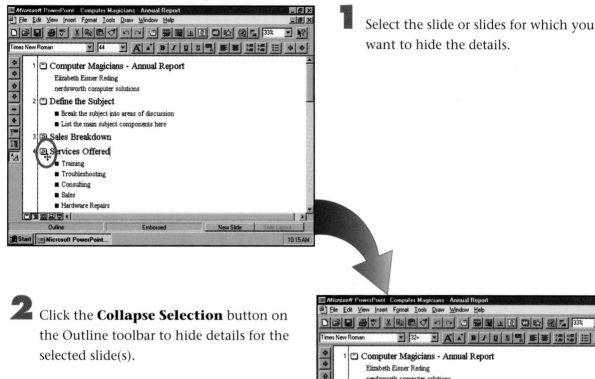

1 Select the slide or slides for which you want to hide the details.

2 Click the **Collapse Selection** button on the Outline toolbar to hide details for the selected slide(s).

> **NOTE** ▼
>
> Unlike other buttons, the Show Titles and Collapse Selection buttons do not appear to be pushed in when they're selected.

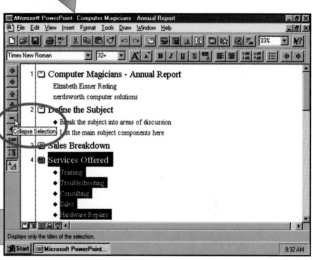

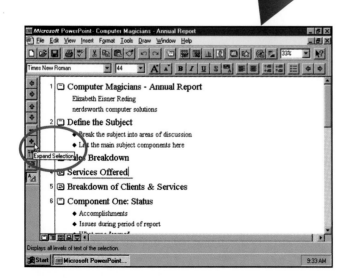

3 PowerPoint indicates that a slide has hidden details by underlining the slide's title. To display the hidden details for the selected slide(s), click the **Expand Selection** button on the Outline toolbar.

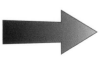

169

4 To hide the details for all the slides in your presentation, click on the **Show Titles** button on the Outline toolbar.

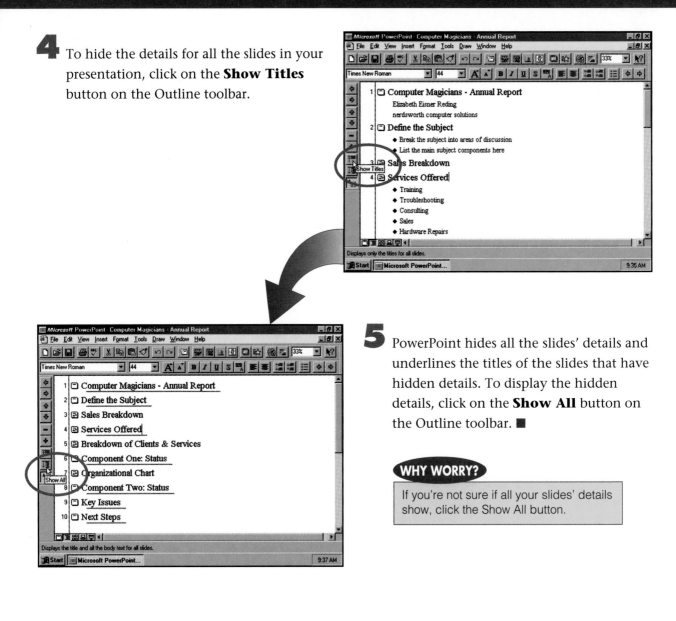

5 PowerPoint hides all the slides' details and underlines the titles of the slides that have hidden details. To display the hidden details, click on the **Show All** button on the Outline toolbar. ■

WHY WORRY?

If you're not sure if all your slides' details show, click the Show All button.

Editing Slide Text

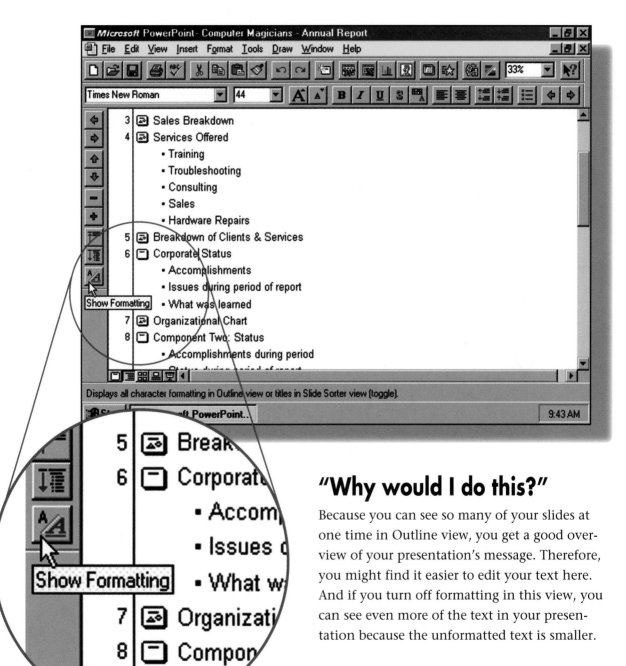

"Why would I do this?"

Because you can see so many of your slides at one time in Outline view, you get a good overview of your presentation's message. Therefore, you might find it easier to edit your text here. And if you turn off formatting in this view, you can see even more of the text in your presentation because the unformatted text is smaller.

1 Click the mouse pointer to place the *insertion point* where you want to change the text in a slide.

NOTE ▼

The insertion point (a flashing vertical line) indicates where the text you type or changes you make will appear.

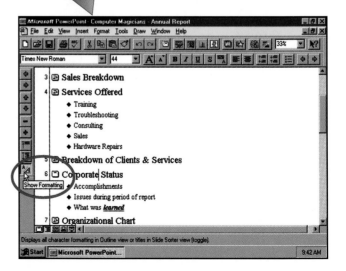

2 Press the **Backspace** key to erase characters to the left of the insertion point; press the **Delete** key to erase characters to the right of the insertion point. Then type in your new text if necessary.

WHY WORRY?

If you have trouble positioning the insertion point in the right location, you can use your arrow keys to move it.

3 To remove character formatting so you can see more slide text on your screen, click on the **Show Formatting** button on the Outline toolbar. PowerPoint hides the formatting and makes all the text look the same. You can turn the formatting back on by clicking the **Show Formatting** button again. ■

Moving Data

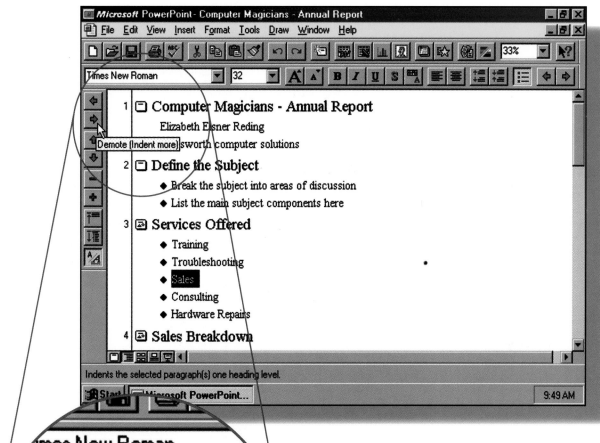

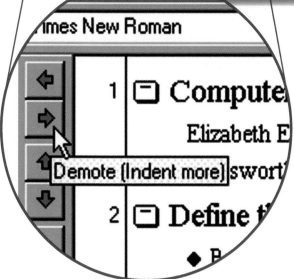

"Why would I do this?"

When you see all the slides together, you may find that some of the slides are in the wrong order or that some bulleted material within a slide should be in another slide. In Outline view, it's easy to change the order of slide text. You can move text up or down and indent it more or less than it already is. You can also change the location of slide text and slides using the drag-and-drop method or the buttons on the Outline toolbar.

1 To move a slide, select it by clicking on its icon with the four-headed arrow pointer.

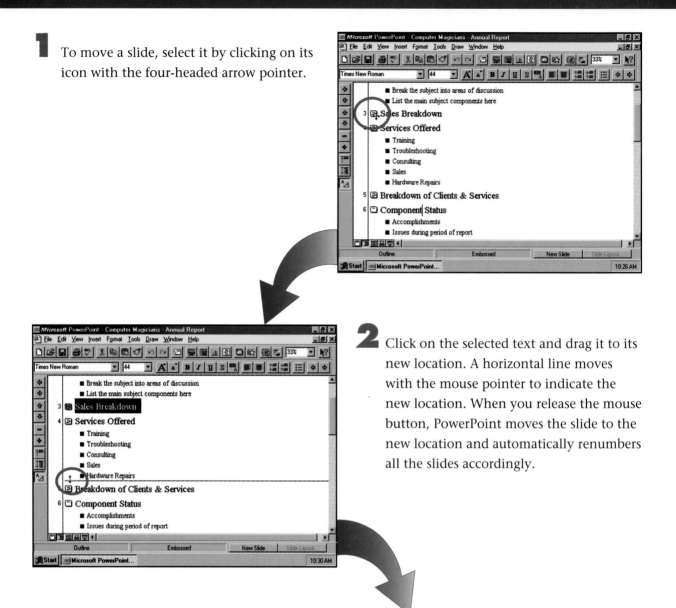

2 Click on the selected text and drag it to its new location. A horizontal line moves with the mouse pointer to indicate the new location. When you release the mouse button, PowerPoint moves the slide to the new location and automatically renumbers all the slides accordingly.

3 To move a bulleted text line, select the text with the four-headed arrow pointer.

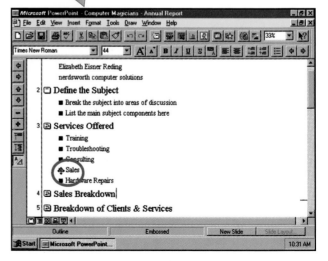

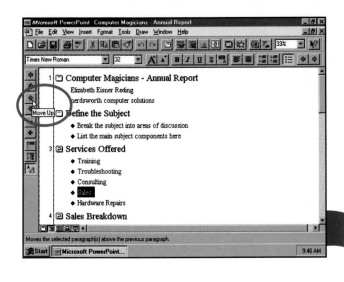

4 To move the text upward in the outline, click the **Move Up** button on the Outline toolbar. The selected text moves up one line. Repeat this as many times as necessary.

5 To move the slide text downward in the outline, click the **Move Down** button on the Outline toolbar as many times as necessary. The selected line moves down one line each time you click the Move Down button.

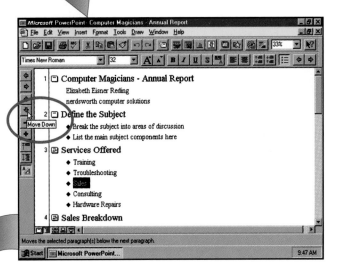

NOTE ▼

By experimenting with the Promote and Demote buttons, you can see if a new slide "works" as its own slide or in a different position.

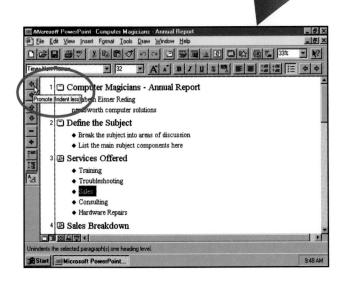

6 To move slide text to a higher level in the outline (to make a bulleted item a separate slide, for example), click the **Promote (Indent less)** button on the Outline toolbar. To move slide text to a lower level, click the **Demote (Indent more)**, button on the Outline toolbar. ∎

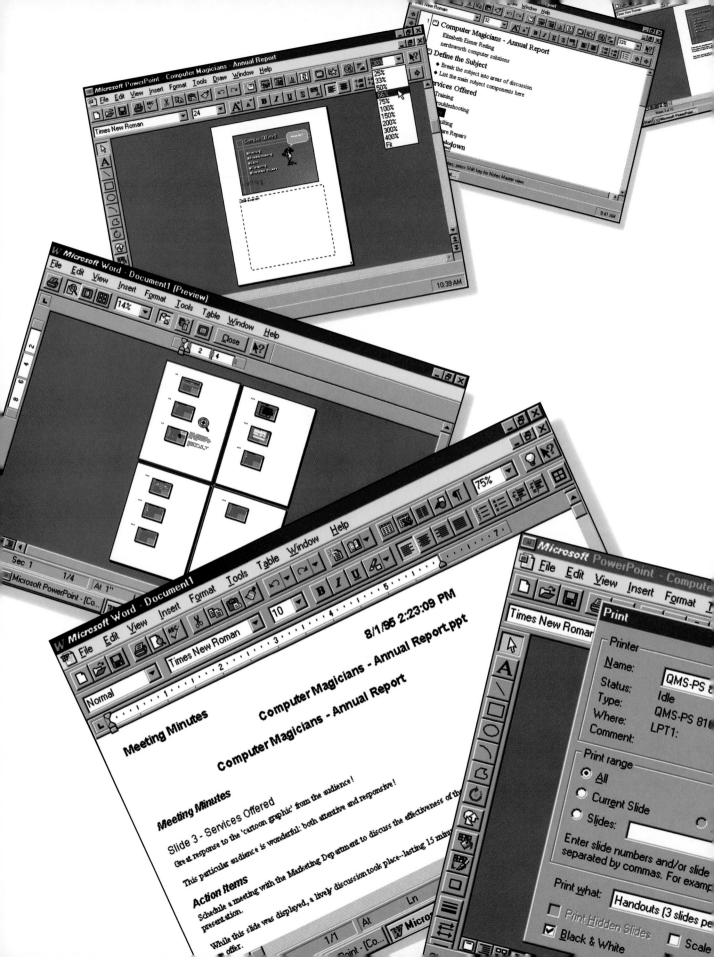

PART VIII

Creating Notes and Handouts

Y ou can't overestimate the importance of your presentation. However, the printed materials you pass out to your audience are of equal importance. If you've ever attended a presentation and wished you had a handout that would help you follow the discussion and on which you could take your own notes, you understand the importance of the tasks in this part.

With PowerPoint, you can print notes (called Speaker's Notes) to help you get through a presentation, and you can create audience handouts to help your audience get through it. An audience handout can include whatever you want: anywhere from one to six slides, an outline, notes you've created, a combination of up to three slides and notes you've created, or a combination of up to three slides and blank lines on which the members of your audience can take their own notes. You can even print *all* of these handouts if you want! Of course, you don't want to inundate your audience with papers, but with the variety of printed material you can produce, you're bound to find several your audience would find helpful.

From another perspective, have you ever wished you could take notes while *giving* a presentation? Wouldn't it be great if you could take your own notes, record official meeting minutes yourself, or create a list of action items (things you personally need to act on when the presentation is over)? Well, this version of PowerPoint contains a powerful tool called the Meeting Minder that enables you to keep a record about your presentation so you can create notes for follow-up after the presentation is over. As long as you have some sort of computer handy— whether it's a notebook or a desktop PC—you can use the Meeting Minder to create useful notes for yourself and others.

You can create Notes, Meeting Minutes, and Action Items for every slide in your presentation. You can create the Notes either in the Notes Pages view or using the Meeting Minder—your choice! And regardless of whether you create your notes in Notes Pages view or the Meeting Minder, you can edit them using either feature. Meeting Minutes tend to be more formal in tone than Notes. Whereas Notes can be humorous observations or reminders of topics you want to discuss, Meeting Minutes are generally observations you record about the slide you're discussing. Action Items are topics that you want to act on at a later time. For example, if a member of your audience asks you for statistical figures to back up a statement in a slide, you can create an Action Item reminding you to send those figures to the person who requested them.

At the conclusion of the presentation, the Meeting Minder creates a summary of its contents using Microsoft Word. You can save and print that summary, as well as a slide containing any Action Items you've created.

In this part, you see the range of printed materials you can create with PowerPoint. You also learn how the use of printed materials can help you and your audience get the most out of a presentation.

In order to use some of these features, such as the handouts and Meeting Minder, you must have Microsoft Word for Windows. Without Word, you can't get the most out of these features.

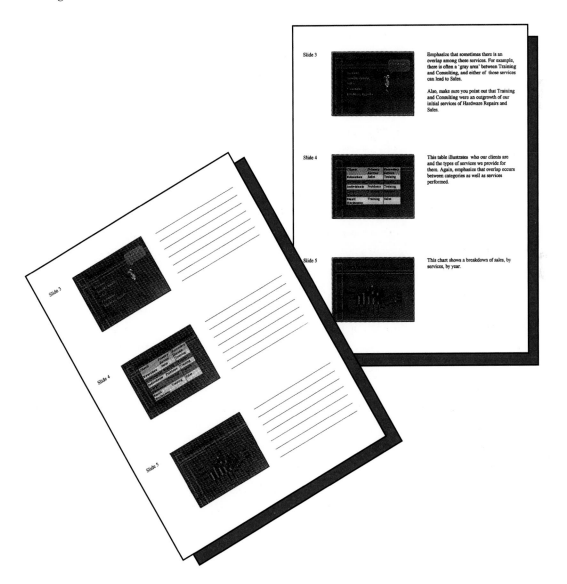

Creating Speaker's Notes

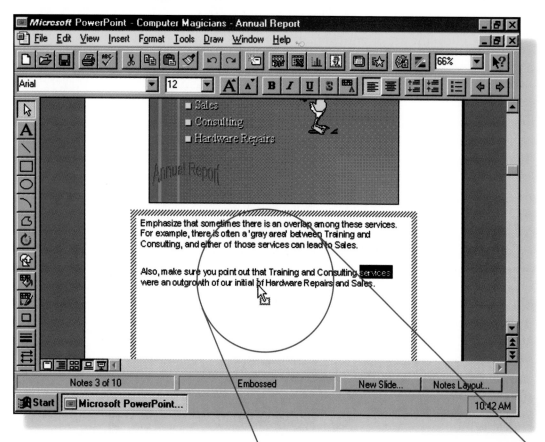

"Why would I do this?"

Remember those mangled index cards that contained the notes you needed to speak in front of your high school class? Although you're better prepared now than you were in high school, you might still need a few notes. Speaker's Notes are printouts on which you can include one or more slides as well as notes for particular slides (which you type directly in the presentation). You can use Speaker's Notes to remind you of important points you want to make or people you want to acknowledge, or for any other notes you want to make to yourself.

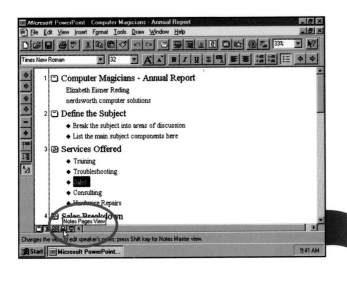

1 From any view, select a slide (or the text in a slide) that you want to make into Speaker's Notes. Then click the **Notes Pages View** button.

2 The Notes Pages view for the selected slide opens. You will enter your notes on the lower half of the page. If the page is too small for you to see the text clearly, click the **Zoom Control** drop-down arrow on the Standard toolbar and select a size that is easier to read.

WHY WORRY?

Setting the Zoom Control to 66% usually does the trick. However, if you still can't read the text, try a higher percentage.

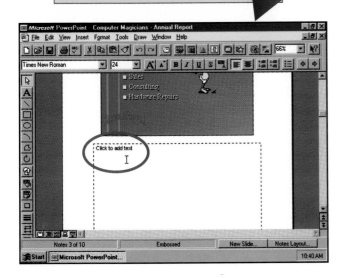

3 Click the **Click to add text** placeholder message on the lower part of the page.

4 The placeholder disappears, and a hatched border and blinking insertion point appear. This means that the area is selected and PowerPoint is ready for your notes.

> **NOTE** ▼
>
> By default, each page of Speaker's Notes contains one slide with the notes printed beneath it. In Task 58, you learn to print the Speaker's Notes in other styles to use as handouts.

5 Type the text for your Speaker's Notes. You can select, edit, and drag-and-drop text just as you would the text in any PowerPoint slide.

> **NOTE** ▼
>
> You can also add, delete, or edit existing Speaker's Notes. Just click on the Notes Pages View button when the slide you want is active.

6 When you want to enlarge or decrease the size of the Speaker's Notes page, click the **Zoom Control** drop-down arrow on the Standard toolbar and select a new size. (The 33% setting gives you a view of the whole page.) ■

> **NOTE** ▼
>
> PowerPoint saves Speaker's Notes with your slides; you do not have to perform additional steps to save them.

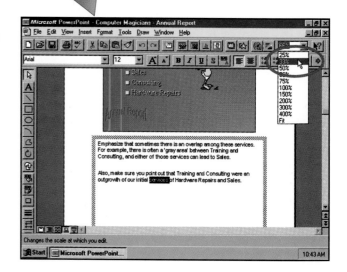

Creating Handouts

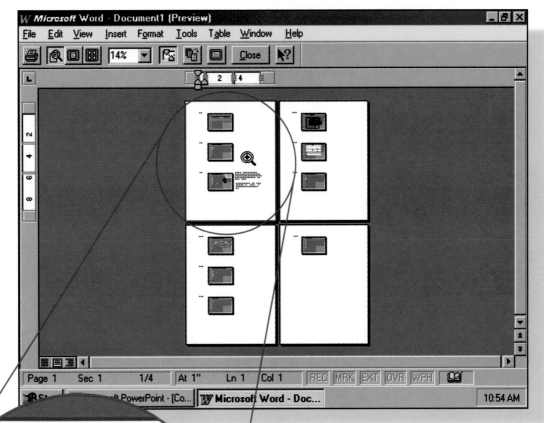

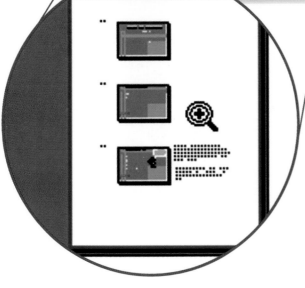

"Why would I do this?"

By creating handouts, you can make your presentation more effective. You can create handouts that contain miniature slides, your Speaker's Notes, blank lines in which viewers can make their own notes, or a combination of these. Has anyone ever given you a handout at a presentation that left you thinking to yourself, "If only I had some room on these sheets to take notes"? Well, when you're at the helm and you're using PowerPoint, it doesn't have to be that way.

1 From any view, open the **Tools** menu and choose **Write-Up**.

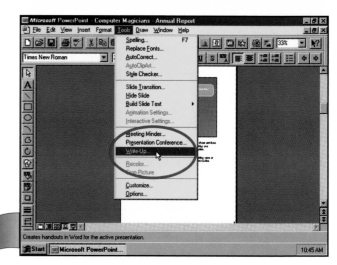

NOTE ▼

In order to create handouts, you must have Microsoft Word for Windows installed on your computer. If you don't have this program installed, the feature doesn't work.

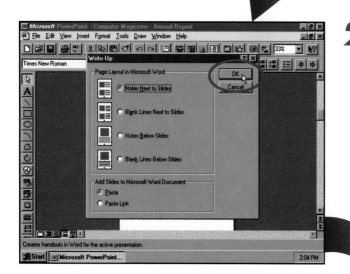

2 The Write-Up dialog box that appears contains four different configurations: two contain prepared notes, and two contain blank lines. Click the option button for the style you want and click **OK**.

WHY WORRY?

If you select one style and then decide later that you prefer another, you can open the Write-Up dialog box again and choose another style.

3 Microsoft Word for Windows opens a new document and places a thumbnail of each slide on as many pages as necessary. These pages reflect the handout style you selected in the Write-Up dialog box, and the notes come from the text you typed in the Notes Pages. (If you haven't typed any notes, Word displays a blank space next to the slide.) To get a better idea of how these pages will look when you print them, click the **Print Preview** button on the Standard toolbar.

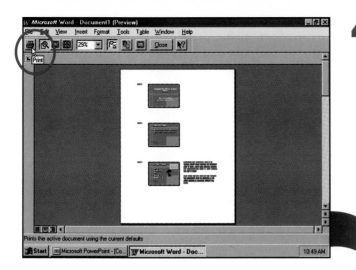

4 Depending on how Word is set up, you may see one preview page or several preview pages. To print out these handouts, click the **Print** button on the Print Preview toolbar.

NOTE

To change the number of pages that are displayed, click the Multiple Pages button on the Print Preview toolbar (the fourth button from the left) and choose the number of pages you want to see.

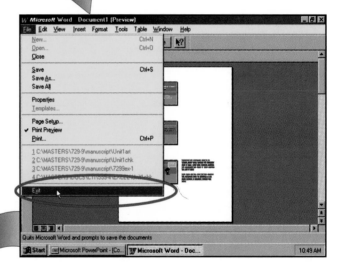

5 To save the handouts, click the **Save** button. Then quit Word by opening the **File** menu and choosing **Exit**. (If you didn't save the handouts first, Word will ask if you want to save the document. Click **Yes** to save the document or **No** to abandon it.)

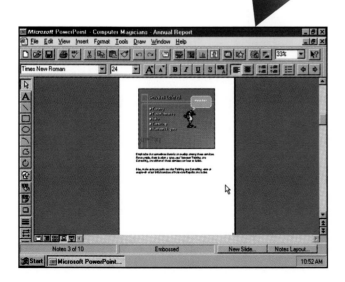

6 PowerPoint reopens, displaying the same slide and view you were in when you chose the Write-Up command. ■

185

Using the Meeting Minder

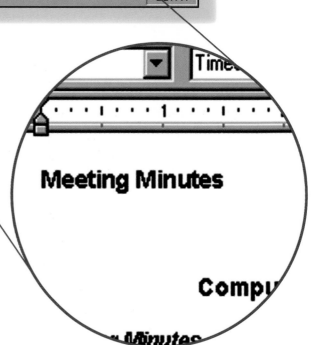

"Why would I do this?"

If you have a habit of forgetting to tell someone something after a meeting or of writing that something down and then losing the paper, you need PowerPoint's Meeting Minder. With Meeting Minder, you can create and add to Notes Pages or take meeting minutes. And you can't lose the paper you write on because PowerPoint saves the Notes Pages with your presentation. Later, you can print out these comments so you can give them to the appropriate persons.

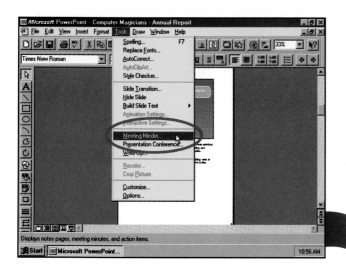

1 From any PowerPoint view, select the slide you want to comment on, open the **Tools** menu, and choose **Meeting Minder**.

NOTE ▼

Each slide has its own Notes Pages, Meeting Minutes, and Action Items, so it's important that you select the correct slide before you open the Meeting Minder.

2 The Meeting Minder dialog box contains tabs for Notes Pages, Meeting Minutes, and Action Items. If theMeeting Minutes tab is at the front of the dialog box, click in the text area and begin typing. Click the **Notes Pages** tab to see any existing Speaker's Notes or to add new notes.

WHY WORRY?

Use the Notes Pages tab to record personal observations you don't want to share. Meeting Minder does not automatically print the Notes Pages.

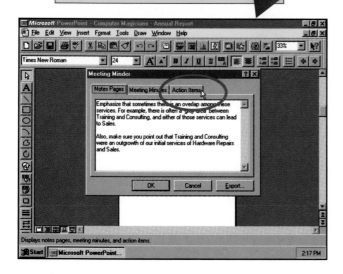

3 PowerPoint displays any existing Speaker's Notes for the active slide in the Notes Pages text area. You can add to or edit these notes by clicking within the text and typing. To take notes on matters you want to take action on later, click the **Action Items** tab.

NOTE ▼

Action Items are like super-reminders telling you to take action.

4 Click within the Action Items text area and type the pertinent information. When you finish entering notes, minutes, and Action Items for the entire presentation and you're ready to print, click the **Export** button. (If the Export button appears grayed out, you haven't entered any Action Items or Meeting Minutes.)

NOTE ▼

To print the Meeting Minder's results, you must have Microsoft Word for Windows installed.

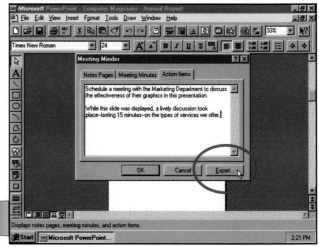

5 In the Meeting Minder dialog box, click the **Send Meeting Minutes and Action Items to Microsoft Word** check box. Then click the **Export Now** button. Word starts and adds the comments about the presentation (except the Notes Pages contents) to a Word document. The Meeting Minder creates a slide at the end of the presentation that contains the Action Items.

6 Click the **Print** button on the Standard toolbar to print the Word document that contains the Meeting Minutes and Action Items. ■

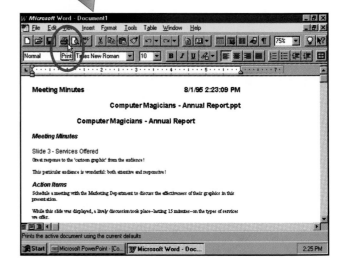

Printing Notes and Handouts

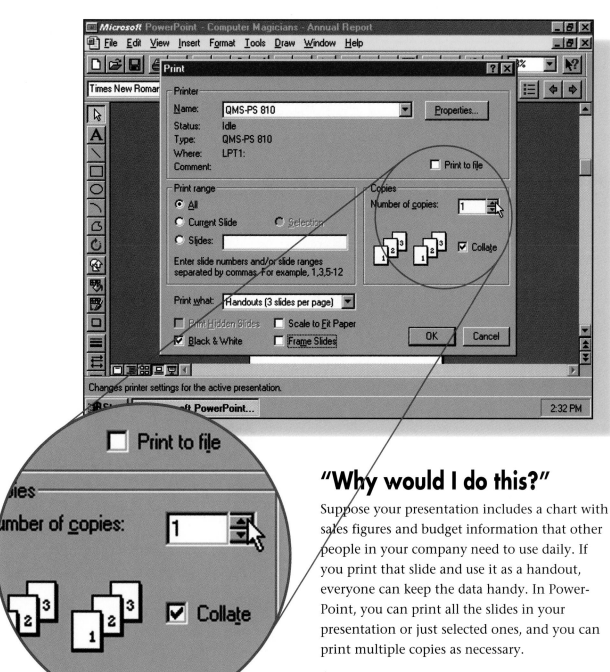

"Why would I do this?"

Suppose your presentation includes a chart with sales figures and budget information that other people in your company need to use daily. If you print that slide and use it as a handout, everyone can keep the data handy. In Power-Point, you can print all the slides in your presentation or just selected ones, and you can print multiple copies as necessary.

1 From any PowerPoint view, open the **File** menu and choose **Print**. The Print dialog box appears.

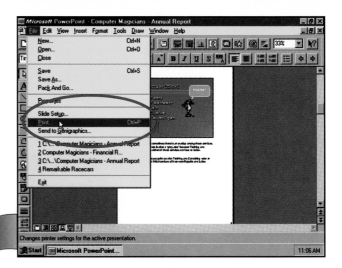

2 Click the **Print what** drop-down arrow and choose the materials you want to print. Specify the slides you want to print in the **Print range** area, and enter the number of copies you want in the **Copies** area.

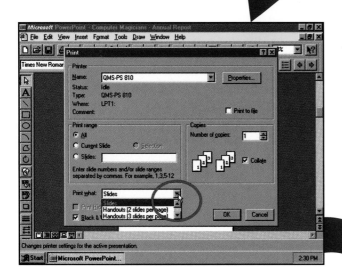

WHY WORRY?

Because PowerPoint offers so many print choices, you should make a list of the types of materials you need to print. For example, you might print handouts with three slides per page, an outline, and a complete set of slides.

3 If you don't have a color printer, you tell PowerPoint to translate your colors to the proper gray tones. To do so, select the **Black & White** check box. If you're finished making selections, click **OK**. ■

NOTE ▼

When you print a color slide in black and white, colors may not print the way you expect. Click the Black & White check box to make sure PowerPoint correctly translates your colors into gray tones.

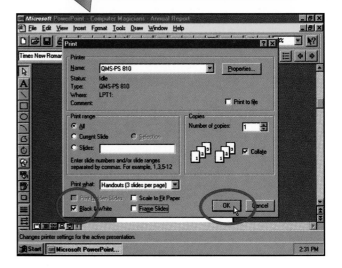

PART IX

Showing a Presentation

Even when you think you're finished with your slides, you'll still find things that need fixing. For instance, after taking a couple of days off from your presentation, you may find that you can improve the order of your slides. Although you can move your slides using the Outline View, you can also change the order of slides using the thumbnails that appear in the Slide Sorter view.

When you finish creating your slides and adding text, artwork, and all the other graphics you need, it's time to turn those slides into a slide show and add special effects. Within a slide show, your slides can contain the following special effects:

Special Effect	Description
Text builds	Display one line of text at a time
Animation effects	Display graphics along with sound effects
Transitions	Control how each slide advances to the next

Each of these special effects adds a different look to your presentation. *Text builds* make each bulleted line of text appear individually. This feature is very effective if you want to focus your audience's attention on the bullet you've covered most recently. In a text build, text can appear from any direction, and it can appear to become dim or a different color when the next line of text appears.

You can apply an *animation effect* to a graphic image and combine it with a sound effect. One animation effect is the "Camera Effect," which makes a sound like a clicking camera shutter while the selected object appears from its center to its outside edges. Of course, your computer needs to be capable of producing sounds in order for these animation effects to work.

A *transition* effect appears on-screen when your show advances from one slide to the next. PowerPoint offers 11 basic types of transitions. However, because you can apply each of these transitions in different directions (for example, from the bottom of the slide, the top, the left, or the right), you have a total of 45 transitions to choose from. You've probably seen a lot of the transition effects before; many local news shows use them during weather broadcasts.

After you perfect your slides and add the appropriate special effects, you're ready to present them. PowerPoint provides you with a number of ways to display your presentation slides. In addition to being able to produce printed materials, you can print your slides on transparencies and display them on an overhead projector. This is a time-honored method of giving a presentation, and although it's not very "hi-tech," it is reasonably priced and available in most businesses. And of course you can display your finished presentation on an ordinary personal computer monitor.

When you run a slide show manually, you advance to the next slide by clicking the mouse button. But what if you want your slide show to run without you? You can add timing to each part of a slide—including the text builds and animation effects—and then program it to run automatically. That way, your slide show can run independently, but you still control the amount of time each slide remains on-screen. You can even "rehearse" your presentation so that you know how long to display each slide (you can tell PowerPoint to display each one for a different amount of time).

And just like in the "good old days" when you showed and wrote on transparencies on an overhead projector, you can "write" notes on your slides using your mouse. The good news about writing on slides is that there's no messy clean-up. However, the notes you write on your slides are temporary; none of them are saved. (Therefore, you shouldn't use this method for taking notes you want to keep. Instead, use the Meeting Minder features discussed in Part VIII.)

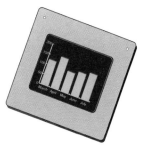

In this part of the book, you learn how to start a slide show and run it manually and automatically. You also learn how to add special effects and graphics to your text.

Changing the Order of Slides

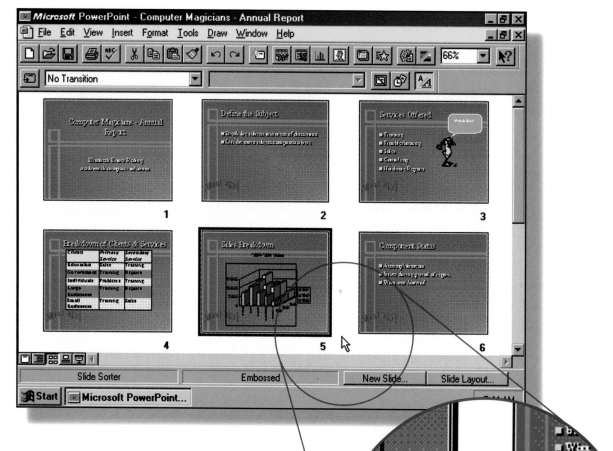

"Why would I do this?"

As you browse through your slides, you may find that you need to change their order. You might decide that moving one of the slides in your presentation will improve the flow from slide to slide, for example. If you move your slides around while you're in the Slide Sorter View, you can examine the thumb-nails for a series of slides and see how each slide relates to the one before it and the one after it.

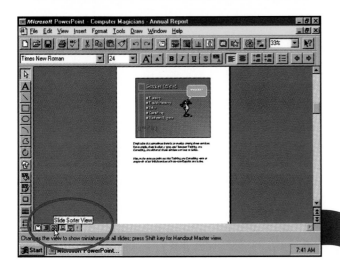

1 From any other view, click the **Slide Sorter View** button to switch to the Slide Sorter view.

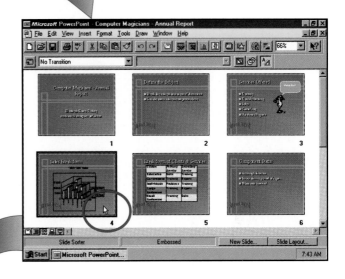

2 If the slide you want to move does not have a dark border around it (indicating that it's selected), click on it. Once you select it, the dark border appears.

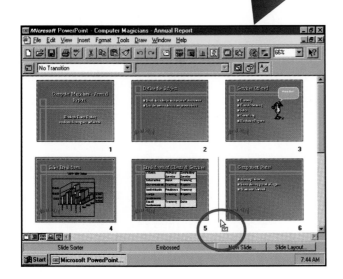

3 Click on the selected slide and drag it to its new location. The drag-and-drop mouse pointer appears, and a vertical line marks the slide's new location. When you're satisfied with the slide's new location, release the mouse button. PowerPoint renumbers the slides accordingly. ∎

WHY WORRY?

If you drag a slide to the wrong location, click the Undo button on the Standard toolbar to reverse the action.

Using Text Builds

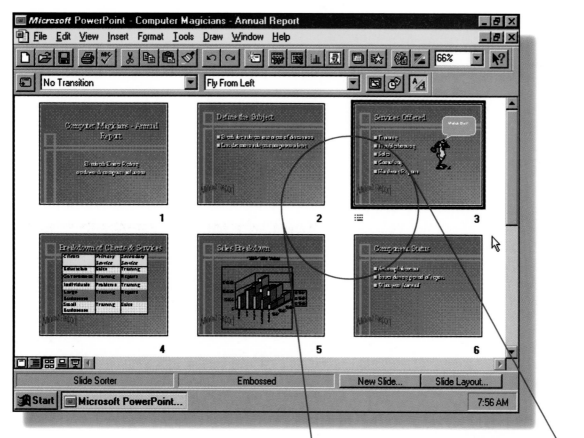

"Why would I do this?"

Have you ever seen a presentation—perhaps at a computer store—where each line of text in a slide becomes dim or another color when another line of text flies onto the screen? That effect is called a *text build*, and it's an effective way for you to keep your viewer's attention on the current text line. You might want to use a text build to create dazzling and professional-looking presentations that will impress your viewers—and maybe your boss, too!

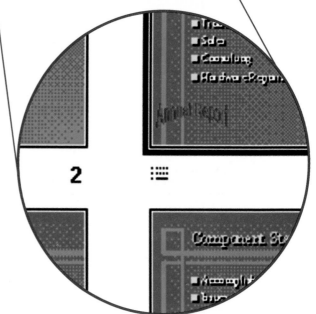

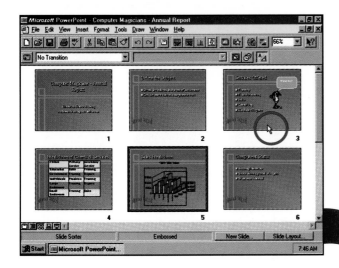

1 From the Slide Sorter View, click on the slide to which you want to add a text build.

2 Open the **Tools** menu, choose **Build Slide Text**, and then choose **Other**. The Animation Settings dialog box appears. It contains the options you use to create a text build.

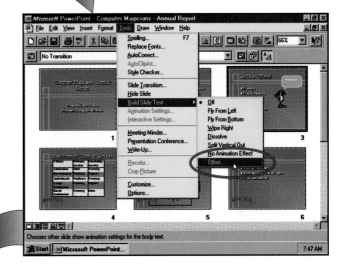

> **NOTE** ▼
>
> You can select any of the text builds in the Build Slide Text submenu. However, choosing Other opens the Animation Settings dialog box. Using the options in this dialog box, you have greater control over how the text build appears.

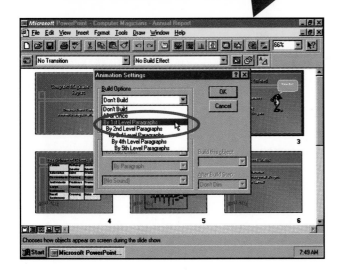

3 Click the **Build Options** drop-down list arrow, and then select the option that describes how you want the text to build. For example, if you select By 1st Level Paragraphs, the text build appears on-screen starting with the least indented bulleted item on the slide. (The levels of text come from the data you typed on your slides or in your outline.)

4 The options in the Effects list control the direction each build comes from and the style it uses. (You've probably seen some of these text builds on your local weather broadcasts.) Click the **Effects** drop-down list arrow, and then click the effect you want to use for your text build.

> **NOTE** ▼
>
> You can build objects as well as text if you're in the Slide View. To do so, select the object you want to build, and then follow these steps. (You learn more about applying effects to objects in Task 63.)

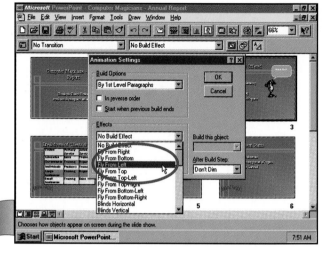

5 If you want a line of text to change color or become dim when the next line appears, click the **After Build Step** drop-down list arrow and select a new color from the list that appears. (Alternatively, you can use the Don't Dim option to make sure text does not dim, or the Hide option to make the text appear to vanish when the next line of text appears.)

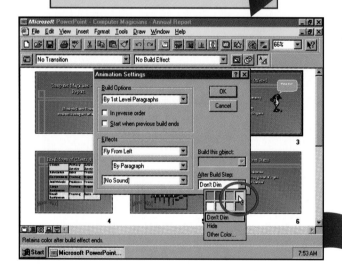

6 After you make all your choices, click **OK**. A special icon appears under the slide's thumbnail in the Slide Sorter View to indicate that the slide uses a text build. ■

> **NOTE** ▼
>
> To preview your text build, click the Slide Show View button (the fifth button from the left above the status bar). PowerPoint starts the slide show from the active slide. Click the mouse button to advance through the text builds.

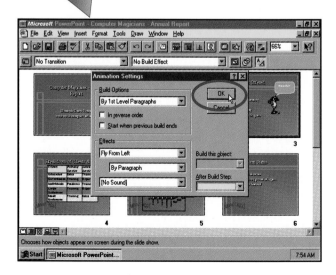

Adding Animation Effects

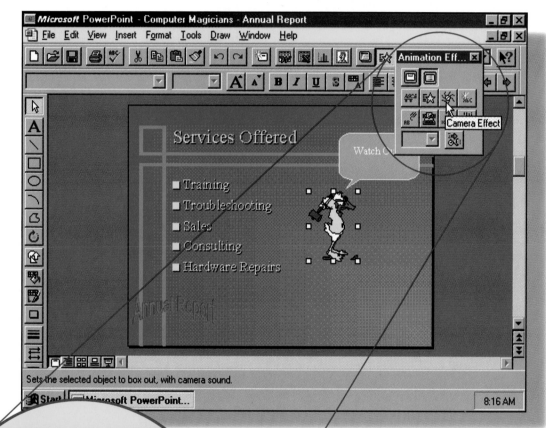

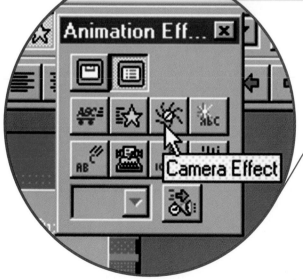

"Why would I do this?"

You can use *animation effects* to make objects appear as your presentation moves from one slide to the next. In addition, if you have a sound card installed in your computer, you will find that most of the animation effects have accompanying sound effects. For example, the Camera Effect makes a sound like a camera shutter. You can use animation effects to set your presentation apart from all the rest.

1 In Slide Sorter View, select the slide to which you want to add an animation effect. Click the **Transition** drop-down list arrow and choose an effect. When the slide show is running, the effect appears with the slide.

WHY WORRY?

Resist the temptation to use every effect in your presentation. Too many transition effects detract from your presentation. The rule of thumb is to use no more than two or three transition effects in one presentation.

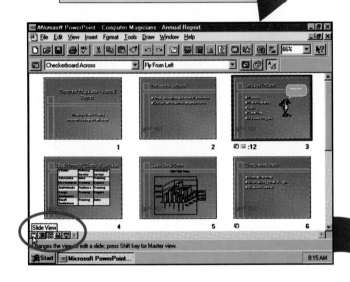

2 An effect icon appears below the thumbnail to indicate that you applied a transition effect to the slide. Click the **Slide View** button so you can assign an animation effect to an object on a slide.

3 Click on the object to which you want to apply an animation effect. Handles appear around the object.

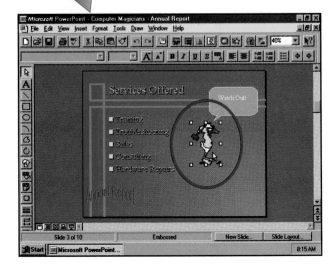

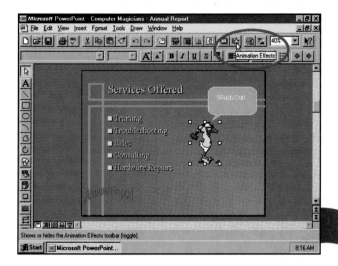

4 Click the **Animation Effects** button on the Standard toolbar. PowerPoint displays the Animation Effects toolbar, which contains buttons for several interesting effects (many of which contain sounds).

5 Click an animation effect button, such as the **Camera Effect** button.

WHY WORRY?

If your computer beeps at you when you click on the animation effect buttons, you probably need to select an object. Click on an object in the slide, and then click the animation effect button.

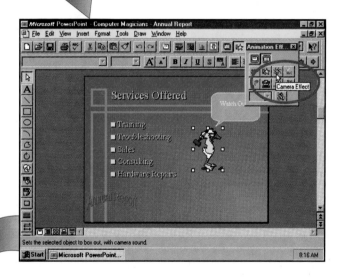

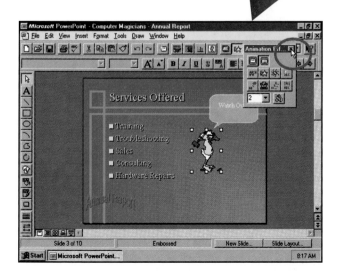

6 After you apply the animation effect, click the **Close** (X) button in the upper-right corner of the Animation Effects toolbar. ■

NOTE ▼

To make the objects in a slide appear in layers during your presentation, click the Animation Order drop-down list arrow after you assign each object an animation effect.

Using Transitions Between Slides

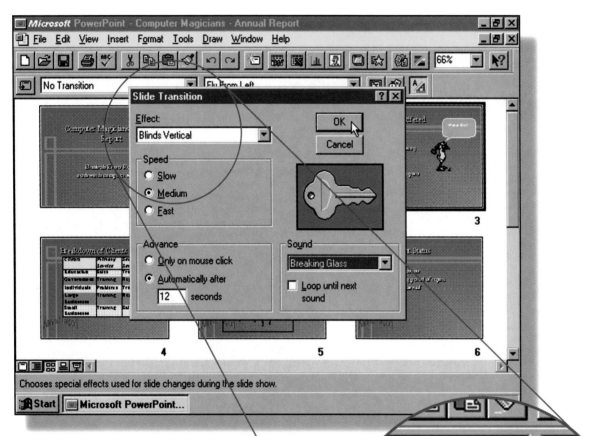

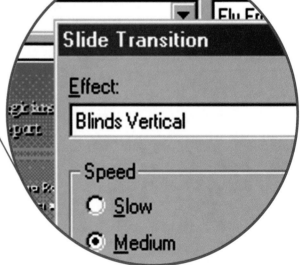

"Why would I do this?"

Special effects make your presentation sparkle, and the way in which one slide advances to the next can add drama to your slides and make you look like a star! You can apply transition effects to make one slide progress smoothly to the next. You can also use certain transitions to "announce" to your viewers that something new is coming up.

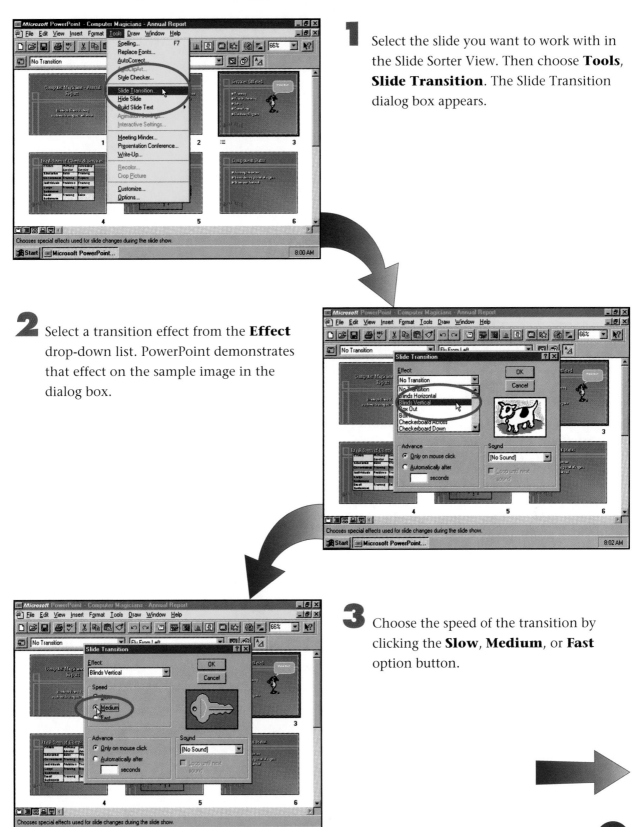

1 Select the slide you want to work with in the Slide Sorter View. Then choose **Tools**, **Slide Transition**. The Slide Transition dialog box appears.

2 Select a transition effect from the **Effect** drop-down list. PowerPoint demonstrates that effect on the sample image in the dialog box.

3 Choose the speed of the transition by clicking the **Slow**, **Medium**, or **Fast** option button.

4 The Advance options enable you to control whether the slides advance automatically or only when you click the mouse. If you choose to have PowerPoint change them automatically, indicate the number of seconds you want the slide to remain on-screen. (Task 66 shows you how to set and rehearse custom timing options.)

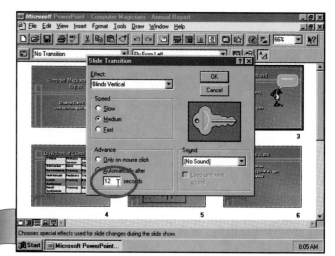

5 Click the **Sound** drop-down list arrow and choose a sound effect to go with the transition. You can set different sounds for different slides (as appropriate for the context of each slide) or no sound at all.

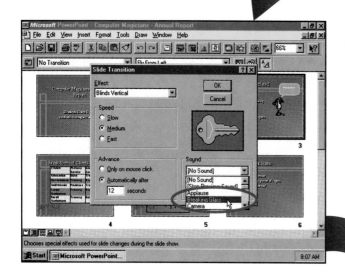

WHY WORRY?

If sound effects don't work, your computer may not be capable of producing sounds. To fix this, you need to install a sound card.

6 When you're satisfied with the transition effect for the selected slide, click **OK**. Repeat the process for each slide to which you want to apply a transition effect. ■

WHY WORRY?

If you decide you don't like a transition you've applied, you're not stuck with it. You can change a transition as many times as you want.

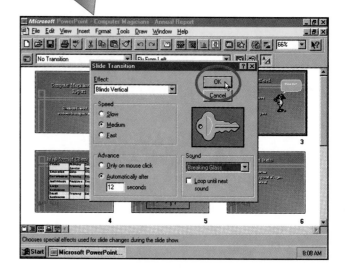

Hiding a Slide

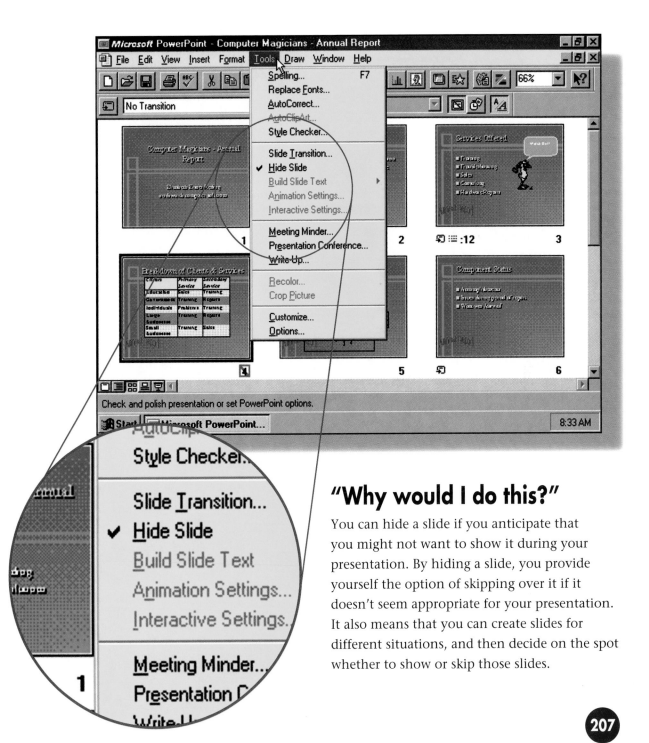

"Why would I do this?"

You can hide a slide if you anticipate that you might not want to show it during your presentation. By hiding a slide, you provide yourself the option of skipping over it if it doesn't seem appropriate for your presentation. It also means that you can create slides for different situations, and then decide on the spot whether to show or skip those slides.

1 From any other view, click the **Slide Sorter View** button to switch to that view.

NOTE ▼

To view a hidden slide during a slide show, press H. Task 67 covers techniques you can use to move between slides.

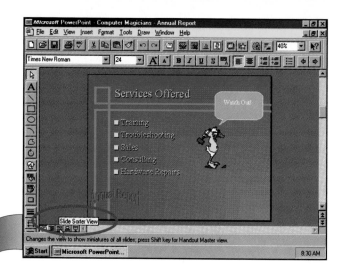

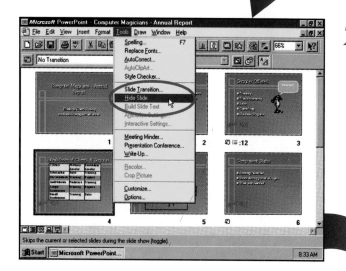

2 Select the slide you want to hide by clicking on it. Then open the **Tools** menu and choose **Hide Slide**. The Hide Slide command toggles between hiding and unhiding a slide; click the command once to turn it on and again to turn it off. When a slide is hidden, a check mark appears to the left of the command.

3 In the Slide Sorter View, PowerPoint displays a slash through the slide number of the hidden slide. ■

WHY WORRY?

If you accidentally tell PowerPoint to hide a slide, open the Tools menu and choose Hide Slide again to turn the option off.

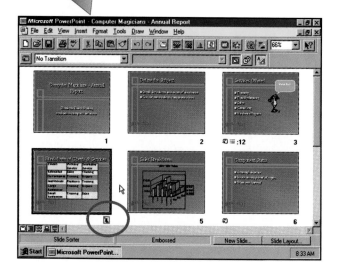

Adding Timing to Slides

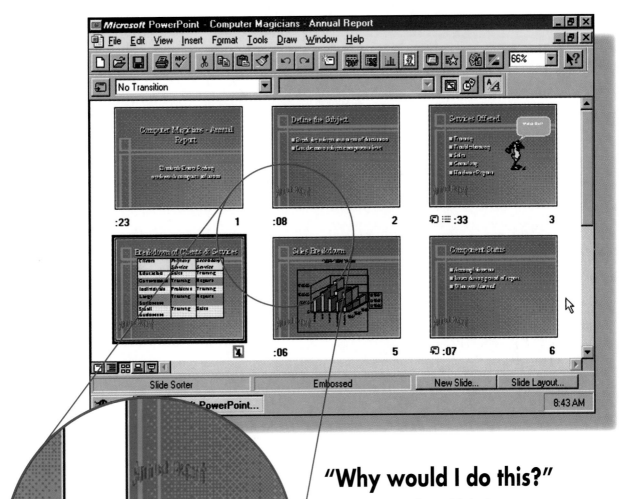

"Why would I do this?"

You might need to add timing to your presentation so that you can run it unattended or with minimal effort. Or, you might add timing to your slides to vary the length of time between text builds, for example, or to make slides with a lot of information remain on-screen longer. When you add timing to your slides, PowerPoint displays the amount of time for each slide under the slide's thumbnail in the Slide Sorter view.

1 From any view, open the **View** menu and choose **Slide Show**. The Slide Show dialog box appears.

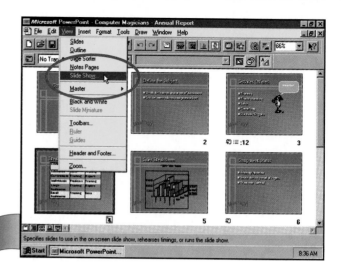

2 Click the **Rehearse New Timings** option button in the Slide Show dialog box.

WHY WORRY?

If you need to change any slide timings later, you must click the Rehearse New Timings option button in the Slide Show dialog box and record new timings.

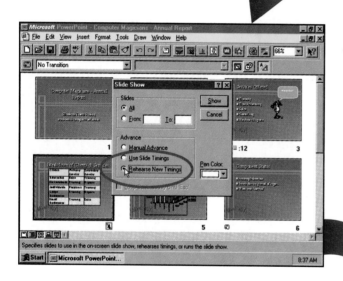

3 Click the **Show** button to start the slide show.

NOTE ▼

You can set your presentation so that PowerPoint runs automatically by clicking the Loop Continuously Until 'Esc' check box in the Slide Show dialog box. (This option is available only if you have selected Manual Advance in the Advance options.)

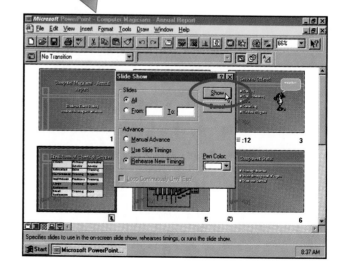

4 The Rehearsal dialog box appears in the lower-right corner of the screen; it keeps track of how much time you spend on each slide. As you rehearse your lines verbally, use the VCR-like buttons in the dialog box to move between slides. Click the **Play** button to advance to the next slide; click the **Pause** button to temporarily stop the timer.

5 After you add timings to all the slides, PowerPoint shows you the total amount of time you need for the presentation. When PowerPoint asks you if you want to record the new slide timings, click **Yes**.

NOTE ▼

During a presentation, you see either a pen or the usual mouse pointer. You learn how to change the pen color in Task 67.

6 PowerPoint applies your new timings to the slides and returns you to the Slide Sorter view. Under each slide, you see the amount of time you allotted for it. ∎

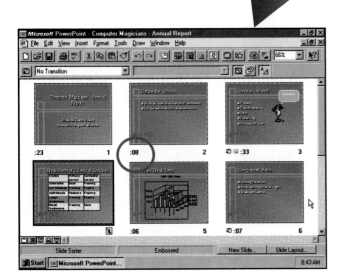

Running a Slide Show

"Why would I do this?"

After you prepare, polish, and rehearse your presentation, the big day comes. It's time to show your presentation to the people for whom you prepared it. You can easily run that professional-quality slide show you've put together with a minimal amount of effort. And you can even write on your slides during the presentation to add emphasis for your viewers.

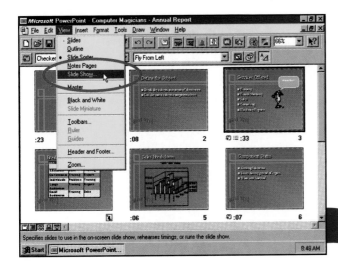

1 From any view, open the **View** menu and choose **Slide Show**. The Slide Show dialog box appears.

2 When the presentation runs, you can add notes to the slides to emphasize points or check off items you've finished discussing. To change the color of the pen, click the **Pen Color** drop-down list arrow and choose a new color.

WHY WORRY?

Any marks you create on a slide are temporary; they disappear when you advance to the next slide.

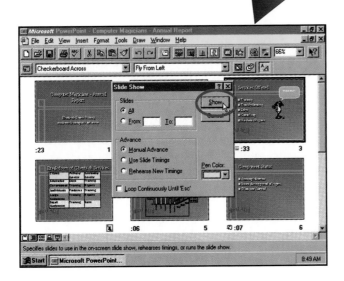

3 Click the **Show** button, and PowerPoint starts the show. If you chose Manual Advance, click the mouse button to advance the slides.

NOTE ▼

To go back to the previous slide during a slide show, press P. To display a hidden slide, press H before the desired hidden slide comes up.

4 At any time during the slide show, you can open a shortcut menu by clicking the button in the lower-left corner of the slide. From the shortcut menu, select **Pen** to turn on the pen (or press **Ctrl+P** to avoid using the mouse or the shortcut menu).

NOTE ▼

The shortcut menu also gives you access to the Meeting Minder feature.

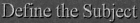

5 The mouse pointer turns into a pen. You can write on a slide by clicking and dragging the pen pointer to create shapes or characters. (The marks you make on a slide are not saved.)

6 When the slide show ends, PowerPoint returns you to the Slide Sorter view. ■

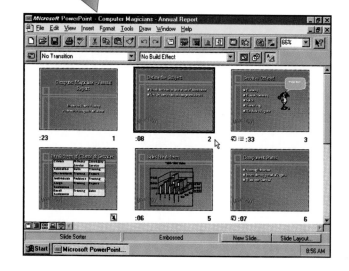

Remarkable Racecars

Our Services Include
- Racecar re-fitting
- Tune-Ups/Getting your vehicle race-ready
- Detailing
- Body work and Repairs
- Engine rebuilding

Remarkable Racecars
always in the *Winner's Circle*

Corporate Structure

Enrico Chavez
Owner & President

Cal Jones
Refitting Specialist

Craig Armbruster

Tony Lee

Jayne Reynolds
Engine Specialist

Ralph Encinas

Marcia Robbins

Robert Yazzie

Raymond Griswold
Detailing Expert

Cindy Elias

Arthur Heinzmann

Bob Foster

Samantha Kelly

Next Year's Anticipated Sales

Service	1st Quarter	2nd Quarter	3rd Quarter	4th Quarter
Re-fits	17,000	15,000	14,000	20,000
Tune-Ups	5,000	4,000	7,000	6,000
Detailing	6,000	4,000	5,000	4,000
Body work	7,000	8,000	7,000	
Engine work	10,000	6,000	5,000	

Anticipated Sales

- Re-fits
- Tune-Ups
- Detailing
- Body work
- Engine work

PART X

Sample Slides

▼ Create a Title Slide

▼ Create a Bulleted List

▼ Create an Organization Chart

▼ Create a Table

▼ Create a Chart

▼ Create a Slide Show

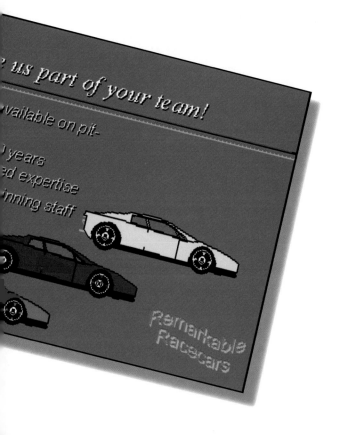

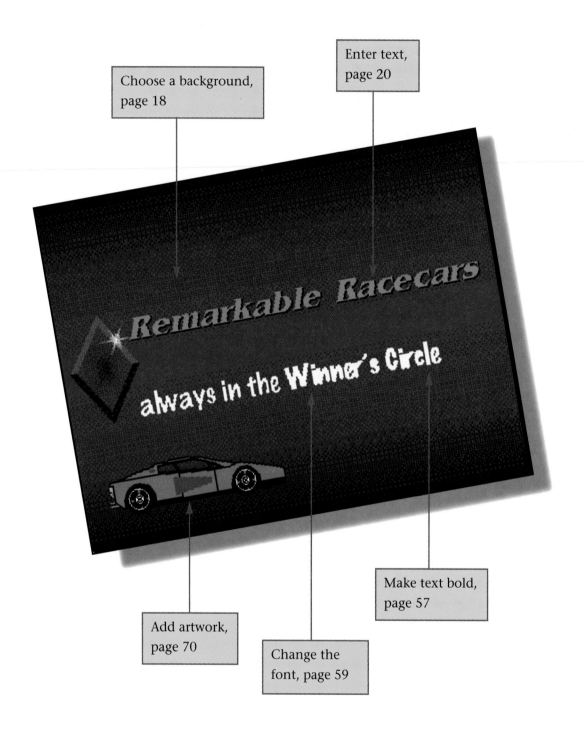

Choose a background, page 18

Enter text, page 20

Make text bold, page 57

Add artwork, page 70

Change the font, page 59

Create a Title Slide

1 Choose a design template for the background of your slide. For help on this step, see this task:

> *Applying a Different Design Template*   Page 18

2 Enter text using the "Click to add text" placeholders. The following task helps:

> *Adding a New Slide*   Page 20

3 Change the appearance and size of text to make the slide look more professional. See the following task:

> *Changing Fonts and Font Sizes*   Page 59

4 Add artwork to a slide to draw attention to the slide. See this task:

> *Inserting Clip Art*   Page 70

5 Call attention to text by making it bold or italic. The following task shows you how:

> *Adding Emphasis to Text*   Page 57

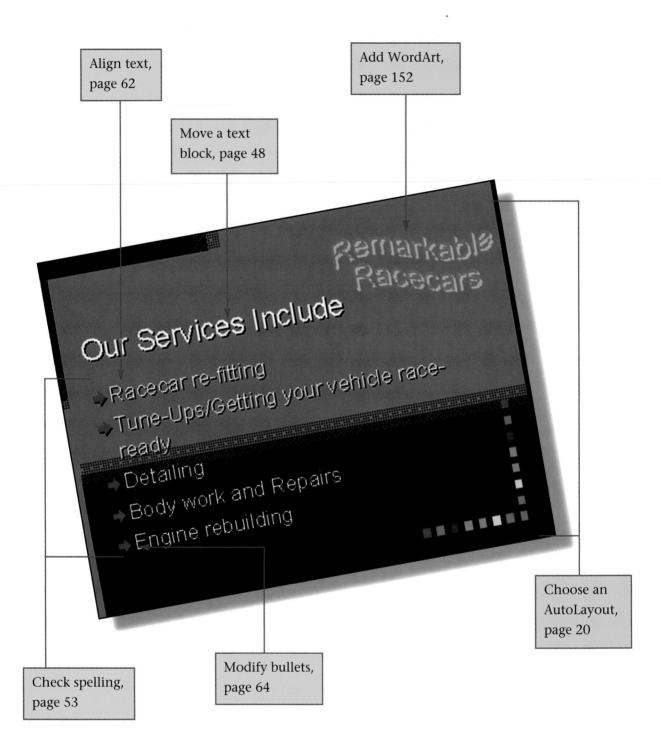

Align text,
page 62

Move a text
block, page 48

Add WordArt,
page 152

Choose an
AutoLayout,
page 20

Check spelling,
page 53

Modify bullets,
page 64

Create a Bulleted List

1 Choose the AutoLayout that's designed for bulleted lists. For help on this step see this task:

Adding a New Slide   *Page 20*

2 Once you enter the slide text, you can change the bullet symbol, as well as its color. The following task can help:

Modifying a Bullet Symbol   *Page 64*

3 You can move any text block on the slide so it's exactly where you want it to be. See this task to help you:

Moving a Text Block   *Page 48*

4 You can change the alignment of characters in a text block, whether they are in a title or a bulleted list. For help, see this task:

Aligning Text   *Page 62*

5 Make sure all the words in your slides are spelled correctly. The following task shows you how:

Checking Spelling   *Page 53*

6 Turn words into works of art using WordArt. These tasks can help you:

Inserting a WordArt Object   *Page 152*

Enhancing WordArt   *Page 156*

Sizing and Moving WordArt   *Page 159*

Move people in an
org chart, page 103

Change relationships
within groups, page 105

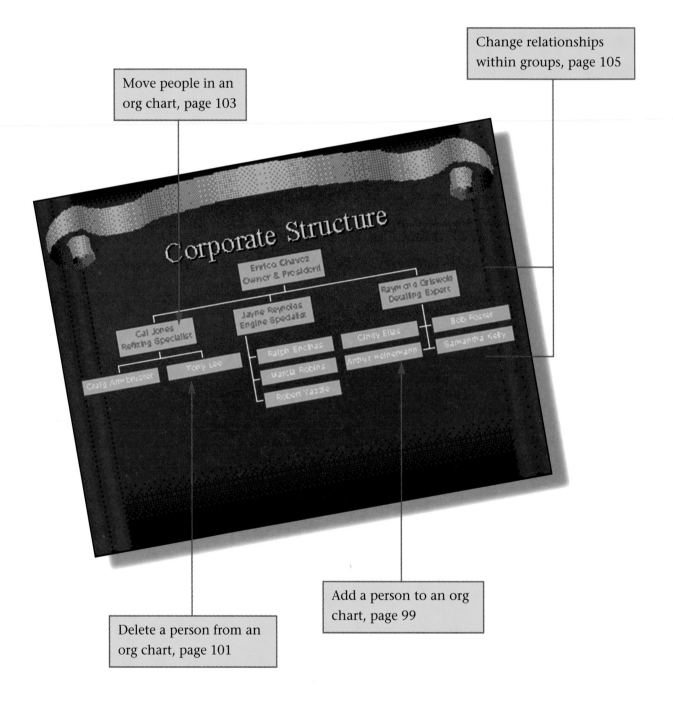

Add a person to an org
chart, page 99

Delete a person from an
org chart, page 101

Create an Organization Chart

1 Add an organization chart to an existing slide, or add a new slide using the AutoLayout for an organization chart. For help on this step see these tasks:

Inserting an Organization Chart on a Slide   *Page 96*

Adding a New Slide   *Page 20*

2 Enter the names and titles for people in the organization. The following task can help:

Adding a Person to an Organization Chart   *Page 99*

3 If necessary, delete people from the chart. See this task to help you:

Deleting a Person from an Organization Chart   *Page 101*

4 Change the way you present the relationships of groups of people in an organization. For help, see this task:

Changing Relationships Within Groups   *Page 105*

5 Once you finish the organization chart, move and resize the chart so it looks great on the slide. The following task shows you how:

Moving an Organization Chart on a Slide   *Page 107*

Sort a table's
contents, page 126

Enter data, page 117

Insert a table,
page 114

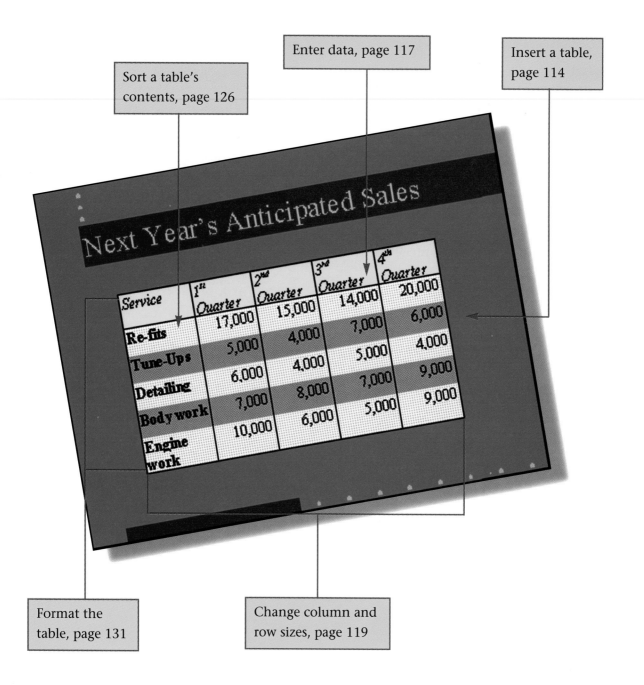

Format the
table, page 131

Change column and
row sizes, page 119

Create a Table

1 Add a table to your chart. For help on this step see this task:

Inserting a Table on a Slide   *Page 114*

2 Enter the data in the table using the mouse and keyboard to move around the table. The following task can help:

Adding Data to a Table   *Page 117*

3 Adjust the column widths and row heights if necessary. See this task to help you:

Changing Column and Row Size   *Page 119*

4 Add or delete columns and rows if necessary. For help, see this task:

Inserting and Deleting a Column or Row   *Page 123*

5 If you want, you can organize the information in your table using the sorting feature. Table data can be sorted using up to three fields and can be in ascending or descending alphabetical order. The following task shows you how:

Sorting Data in a Table   *Page 126*

6 Add beautiful formatting to a table. This task can help you:

Using the Table AutoFormat Feature   *Page 131*

Modify chart text, page 143

Change a chart type, page 149

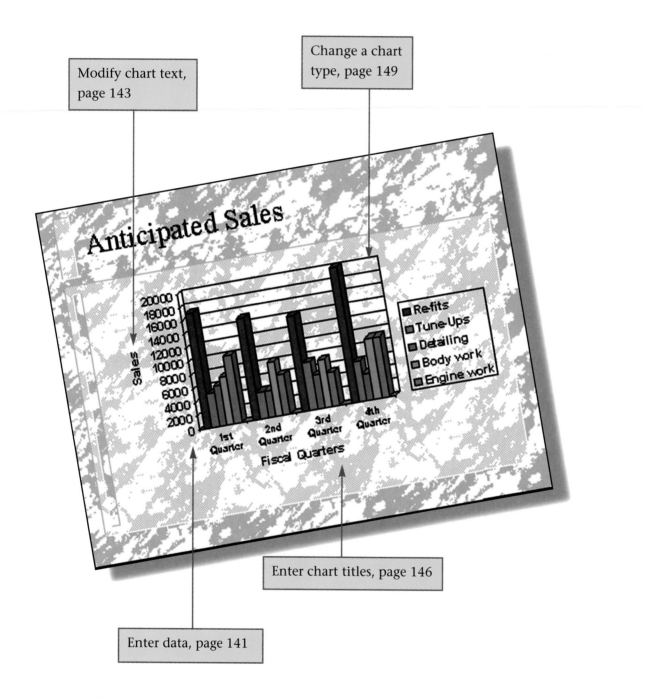

Enter chart titles, page 146

Enter data, page 141

Create a Chart

1 Add a chart to a slide. For help on this step see this task:

> *Inserting a Chart on a Slide*   *Page 138*

2 Enter data in the chart and modify the chart text if necessary. The following tasks can help you:

> *Adding Chart Data*   *Page 141*
>
> *Modifying Chart Text*   *Page 143*

3 After you enter the data, you may want to add titles to the chart. For help, see this task:

> *Adding a Chart Title*   *Page 146*

4 Change the chart type to best fit your data. See this task to help you:

> *Changing the Chart Type*   *Page 149*

Run the show,
page 212

Hide a slide,
page 207

Add text builds,
page 198

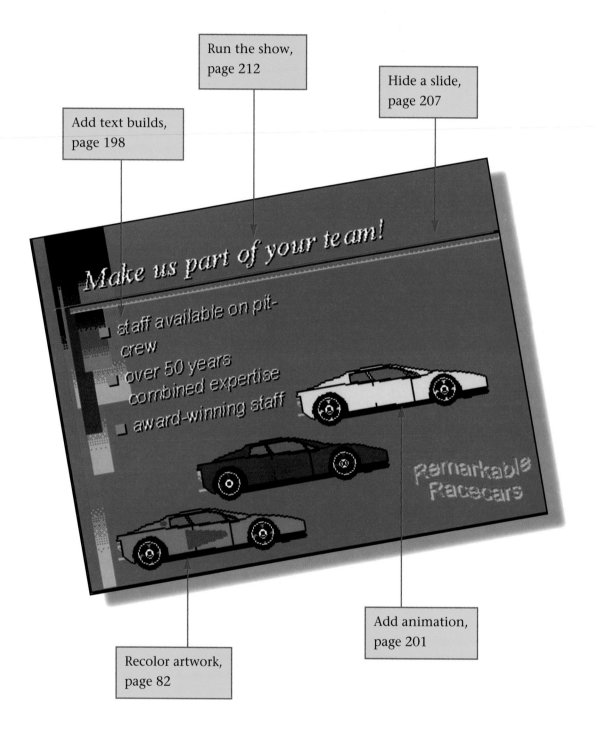

Recolor artwork,
page 82

Add animation,
page 201

Create a Slide Show

1 Create text builds so text appears one line at a time. For help on this step see this task:

> *Using Text Builds*   *Page 198*

2 Recolor a graphic image so the colors look exactly the way you want them to.

> *Recoloring Clip Art*   *Page 82*

3 Graphic images can appear on a slide with special animation effects. The following task can help:

> *Adding Animation Effects*   *Page 201*

4 Hide slides so you have them on hand if you decide to show them at the last minute. See this task to help you:

> *Hiding a Slide*   *Page 207*

5 Add timing as well as text builds and animated graphics to individual slides. For help, see this task:

> *Adding Timing to Slides*   *Page 209*

6 Present your slide show, moving forward and back among slides using your mouse and keyboard. The following task shows you how:

> *Running a Slide Show*   *Page 212*

Quick Reference

If you cannot remember how to access a particular PowerPoint feature, use this list to find the appropriate command and shortcut key.

Feature	Menu, Command	Shortcut Key
Action Items	Tools, Meeting Minder (Action Items tab)	(none)
Clip Art	Insert, Clip Art	(none)
Close File	File, Close	(none)
Copy	Edit, Copy	Ctrl+C
Cut	Edit, Cut	Ctrl+X
Delete Slide	Edit, Delete Slide	(none)
Exit PowerPoint	File, Exit	Alt+F4
Find	Edit, Find	Ctrl+F
Font	Format, Font	(none)
Help	Help	F1
Hide Slide	Tools, Hide Slide	(none)
Master Slide	View, Master, Slide Master	(none)
Meeting Minutes	Tools, Meeting Minder (Meeting Minutes tab)	(none)
Move	Edit, Cut and then Edit, Paste	Ctrl+X, then Ctrl+V
New File	File, New	Ctrl+N
New Slide	Insert, New Slide	Ctrl+M
Notes Pages	Tools, Meeting Minder (Notes Pages tab)	(none)
Object	Insert, Object	(none)
Open File	File, Open	Ctrl+O
Paste	Edit, Paste	Ctrl+V
Print	File, Print	Ctrl+P
Redo	Edit, Redo	Ctrl+Y

Feature	Menu, Command	Shortcut Key
Replace	Edit, Replace	Ctrl+H
Save As	File, Save As	(none)
Save	File, Save	Ctrl+S
Select All	Edit, Select All	Ctrl+A
Slide Layout	Format, Slide Layout	(none)
Slide Transition	Tools, Slide Transition	(none)
Spelling	Tools, Spelling	F7
Text Alignment	Format, Alignment	(none)
Undo	Edit, Undo	Ctrl+Z
Write-Up	Tools, Write-Up	(none)

Toolbar Guide

The following tables show the buttons on the PowerPoint toolbars that you use most often. Not all of the toolbars appear in all four views (Slide view, Outline view, Slide Sorter view, and Notes Pages view). Therefore, each table indicates in which view the toolbar appears.

Standard Toolbar (All Views)

Button	Name	Description
	New	Creates a new presentation
	Open	Opens a presentation
	Save	Saves a presentation
	Print	Prints a presentation
	Spelling	Checks the spelling in a presentation
	Cut	Cuts the selected text or object from the slide and places it in the Clipboard
	Copy	Copies the selected text or object and places the copy in the Clipboard

Button	Name	Description
	Paste	Pastes the contents of the Clipboard to the slide
	Format Painter	Copies the attributes of the selection
	Undo	Reverses the effect of the last operation
	Redo	Reverses the effect of Undo
	Insert New Slide	Inserts a new slide
	Insert Microsoft Word Table	Inserts a Word table
	Insert Microsoft Excel Worksheet	Inserts an Excel worksheet
	Insert Graph	Opens Microsoft Graph
	Insert Clip Art	Opens the Microsoft ClipArt Gallery
	Apply Design Template	Applies a different design template
	Animation Effects	Applies special effects to objects
	Report It	Exports a PowerPoint outline to Word
	B&W View	Changes slide colors to shades of gray
33%	Zoom Control	Makes images larger or smaller
	Help	Gives helpful information on a variety of topics (open the Help menu or press F1 for help on a specific topic)

Formatting Toolbar (All Views)

Button	Name	Description
Times New Roman	Font Face	Changes the font of the selection
24	Font Size	Changes the font size of the selection (you specify the size)
A	Increase Font Size	Makes the font larger
A	Decrease Font Size	Makes the font smaller
B	Bold	Makes characters bold
I	Italic	Makes characters italic
U	Underline	Makes characters underlined
S	Text Shadow	Adds a shadow to characters
A	Text Color	Changes text color
≡	Left Alignment	Aligns text with the left margin
≡	Center Alignment	Aligns text between the two margins
≡	Increase Paragraph Spacing	Increases spaces between paragraphs
≡	Decrease Paragraph Spacing	Decreases spaces between paragraphs
≔	Bullet On/Off	Turns on/off automatic insertion of bullets in lists
◄	Promote (Indent less)	Makes text more important
►	Demote (Indent more)	Makes text less important

Slide Viewer Toolbar (All Views)

Button	Name	Description
	Slide View	Displays only the selected slide
	Outline View	Displays slide text only—no graphics
	Slide Sorter View	Displays miniature versions of all the slides
	Notes Pages View	Displays a miniature slide above a text area in which you can type notes
	Slide Show	Shows the slides with all special effects

Drawing Toolbar (Notes Pages View and Slide View)

Button	Name	Description
	Selection Tool	Selects a slide object or text box
	Text Tool	Creates a new text box
	Line Tool	Draws a straight line
	Rectangle Tool	Draws a rectangle or square shape
	Ellipse Tool	Draws a circle or oval shape
	Arc Tool	Draws an arc (or curved line)
	Freeform Tool	Draws a shape that you design
	Free Rotate Tool	Rotates an existing slide object
	AutoShapes	Displays a palette containing predesigned shapes you can drag onto a slide
	Fill Color	Assigns a color to the interior of a shape
	Line Color	Assigns a color to an existing line

Drawing Toolbar (Notes Pages View and Slide View)

Button	Name	Description
	Shadow On/Off	Turns shadow characteristic on or off
	Line Style	Changes the weight of an existing line
	Arrowheads	Changes or adds arrowheads to an existing line
	Dashed Lines	Changes the style of a dashed line

View Outline Toolbar (Outline View)

Button	Name	Description
	Promote (Indent less)	Makes text more important
	Demote (Indent more)	Makes text less important
	Move Up	Moves a line upward in the outline
	Move Down	Moves a line downward in the outline
	Collapse Selection	Hides outline details in the active slide (usually the text within the slide)
	Expand Selection	Shows outline details in the active slide
	Show Titles	Hides outline details for all slides
	Show All	Shows outline details for all slides
	Show Formatting	Hides/Shows formatting attributes in the outline

View Slide Sorter Toolbar (Slide Sorter View)

Button	Name	Description
	Slide Transition	Adds or changes the transition speed or adds a sound to a transition
No Transition ▼	Slide Transition Effects	Displays a drop-down list of transition effects
No Build Effect ▼	Text Build Effects	Displays a drop-down list of text build effects
	Hide Slide	Creates a hidden slide that you can skip over during a slide show
	Rehearse Timings	Sets the length of time each slide remains on-screen during a presentation
	Show Formatting	Turns formatting (such as colors, text, and graphics) on and off

Glossary

3-D   Three-dimensional. In reference to some chart types such as column, bar, and pie, this describes the shadow effects Microsoft Graph adds to the charts to make the charts look as if they have depth.

Action Items   The feature that enables you to compile a list of items you want to remember and respond to by doing something. An example of an action item is "Follow up on this next week by asking Mr. Jones the results of his survey. Distribute the findings in the monthly memo to the Board of Directors." You can create action items during a presentation; you just jot down ideas as you think of them. The Meeting Minder compiles all action items into a new slide at the end of your presentation.

Animation Effects   A special transition that you can apply to a single object within a slide. Generally, these effects include sound. You apply Animation Effects with a button on the Standard toolbar.

attribute   A quality or characteristic you apply to text, charts, tables, and so on. An attribute of text might be its font or size; an attribute of a chart might be the color or line width of a feature.

AutoLayout   One of PowerPoint's predesigned slides to which you can add your own text. Each AutoLayout contains placeholders and formatting for items within the specific layout. Examples of AutoLayouts include a Title slide and Bulleted List slide.

build (**text**)   An effect you can apply to text so that the items in a bulleted list appear on-screen one at a time. You have the options to build the bulleted lists by paragraph, word, or character and to dim each line when PowerPoint introduces the next line.

bullet   A symbol such as a large dot, check mark, or small box that you place at the beginning of each item in a list. A bullet emphasizes the items in the list; each item in a bulleted list is equally important.

Bulleted List   One of PowerPoint's AutoLayouts; it is preformatted to include a list of equally important items.

cell   Area in a table or datasheet in which you enter data; the intersection of a column and a row.

chart   A visual representation of data you enter in a datasheet. Also known as a graph.

check box   An option you use to turn a feature on or off. When you click in a check box, a check mark appears in the check box, and PowerPoint turns the feature on. You turn a check box off by clicking it again to remove the check mark.

"Click to add text"   Placeholder text that appears on a slide to indicate where you can enter text. If you click this placeholder, a dotted outline box appears on-screen for you to type your text in.

Clipboard   A Windows feature in which your programs temporarily store information that you've copied or cut. In most cases, you can paste information into your slide from the Clipboard as many times as you want until you place new data on the Clipboard.

column   In a table, the vertical division of the text or numbers.

copy   To duplicate text or objects. When you copy an item, your program places the copy on the Windows Clipboard, and the original item remains intact. You can use the Copy button on the Standard toolbar to copy.

cut   To remove text or objects from their original locations. When you cut an item, PowerPoint removes the original item and places it on the Clipboard. You can use the Cut button on the Standard toolbar to cut items.

data   Numbers or text you enter into a table or chart.

default   A setting or option that PowerPoint uses if you don't choose something else. When you select a command or open a dialog box, the setting or option that's already selected is the default. Usually, it's the choice most people are likely to make. If you want to choose something other than the default choice, you have to specify it in the dialog box.

demote   To indent a text line more so that it appears in a less prominent position in the slide show outline.

design template   One of a series of predesigned slide designs that include colors, patterns, fonts, and formatting. You can apply a design template at any time by clicking on the Design Template button on the Standard toolbar.

double-click   To click the left mouse button twice quickly. In a dialog box, double-clicking a button is the same as clicking the button and clicking OK.

drag-and-drop   A method you can use to move selected information from one location to another without going through the cut-and-paste process; drag-and-drop is much faster and more efficient. When you use this feature, you see the drag-and-drop mouse pointer.

Drawing toolbar   A set of buttons you can use to draw objects such as lines, arrowheads, circles, and rectangles.

format   To assign characteristics to text, paragraphs, charts, pages, and so on. For example, you can apply bold formatting to make text stand out more.

Formatting toolbar   The second toolbar on the PowerPoint screen (under the Standard toolbar). This toolbar contains buttons you can use to format characters in slides by changing fonts and font sizes, applying bold, and changing the alignment of characters (to name a few).

graph   *See* chart.

handles   Small squares that surround an object or text block when you select it. You can click on a handle and drag it to resize the object or text block.

Help   The menu whose commands you can use to access the online Help system, which contains information on a variety of subjects. In addition to using the Help menu, you can press F1 anytime you need help.

I-beam   The standard mouse pointer's appearance when it is in a text block. When you see this mouse pointer (which looks like a capital letter I), you can enter or edit text at that position. If you want to move it somewhere else, just click on that spot.

justification   The alignment of text relative to the left and right margins. When you justify text, PowerPoint inserts spaces of varying sizes between the words so that every line in the paragraph has the same width.

label   Text or numbers (such as years or corporate departments) that you do not use for calculations.

legend   Text and a sample pattern, symbol, or color you can use to show how you represent data in a chart. A legend is usually in a box.

logo   Text or artwork that symbolizes a company or product. Advertising campaigns use logos frequently to inspire name recognition with a product. Companies often use logos as "brand marks" for their products or services. You can use the WordArt program to insert a logo on your slides.

Meeting Minder   A feature that enables you to create Speaker's Notes, Action Items, and Meeting Minutes. The Meeting Minder records information from individual slides and saves the information within the presentation. You can then print out the Speaker's Notes and Meeting Minutes using Microsoft Word for Windows. Meeting Minder places your Action Items on a new slide that it adds to the end of the presentation.

Meeting Minutes Information that you record during a presentation about individual slides.

menu A list of commands from which you can choose. The File menu, for example, contains file-related commands such as Open, Close, and Exit.

menu bar The horizontal strip near the top of the screen that contains available menus (which contain commands).

Notes Pages view The view you use when you give a presentation (it includes Speaker's Notes). Notes Pages view can contain one or several thumbnails (small pictures of slides), depending on how you choose to print them out.

object A text block or graphic image that you can move, copy, or resize. When you click an object once, handles surround the object. These handles enable you to resize or move the item.

option button An element (usually in a dialog box) that you use to make a selection. Click an option button to choose the corresponding option. You can select only one option button at a time; PowerPoint automatically deselects the previously selected button when you select a new one.

organization chart A diagram that you use to illustrate the structure of a group of people. To use this feature, you need to install Microsoft Organization Chart (which comes with PowerPoint) on your computer.

Outline view Shows each slide and its details without the graphics. You can collapse or expand information in slides depending on how much information you want to see. Using the Outline toolbar buttons, you can promote or demote slides by changing the amount of indentation used within slides, and you can change the order of slides within the presentation.

paste To place the contents of the Clipboard in a new location. You can paste text or objects with the Paste button on the Standard toolbar.

placeholder Dummy text or boxes that you replace with text, a table, a chart, or a graphic image. AutoLayout slides come with placeholders that you can replace with your own information.

presentation The body of work you create in PowerPoint, which consists of one or more slides and other materials you use to assist you in a giving a speech. PowerPoint considers a "presentation" to be made up of both the file that contains your slides and the physical act of presenting the slides to a group of people.

promote To indent a text line less so that the line is more prominent in your slide show outline.

recolor To change the colors in a clip art image.

Redo   A command that enables you to reverse the last action or command on which you used the Undo command. You can also use Redo to repeat a command you just used. The Standard toolbar includes a Redo button.

resize   To change the size of an object by selecting it and dragging one of its handles.

save   In order to use your work at a later date, you need to store it within your computer (on your hard disk or on a floppy diskette). You save your work using the Save button on the Standard toolbar.

scroll bars   Gray horizontal and vertical bars that appear on-screen and in dialog boxes and drop-down lists, usually along the edge of the screen or at the edge of the item in the dialog box or list. Scroll bars enable you to see screen areas or choices that are hidden from view. Scroll bars appear only when there is more information available than is visible on-screen.

select   To choose an object or text so that PowerPoint knows what you want to work with. Click on an object or text block to select it, and handles appear around the item. In most cases, you must select text or an object before you can move, copy, edit, or resize it.

slide   Each independent idea within a presentation comprises a slide. Each slide appears on your computer monitor in the shape of a 35mm slide (even if you don't create 35mm slides for your presentation).

Slide Show view   The view in whichall the slides in the presentation, including transitions, animation effects, hidden slides, and text builds, appear on-screen. During a slide show, each slide fills the screen, and no menus or toolbars appear. You can show slide shows manually by controlling the show with your mouse or automatically so that PowerPoint shows the slides in a continuous loop until you press the Esc key.

Slide Sorter view   The view that shows all the slides in your presentation in miniature versions. You can use this view to apply transitions and reorganize the slides.

Slide view   Shows a single slide on your computer screen. This is the view you use to work with the clip art and the details of the individual slides.

sort   To change the order of information in a table. You can sort information alphabetically or numerically and in ascending or descending order.

Speaker's Notes   Your comments that appear on the Notes Pages. These notes can be as formal or informal as you want. Speaker's Notes basically replace the index cards you may have used in previous presentations.

Spelling Checker   A feature that searches your slides for misspellings. Check spelling using the Spell Check button on the Standard toolbar.

Standard toolbar   The first toolbar on the PowerPoint screen (it appears below the title bar at the top of your screen). This toolbar contains buttons you can use to perform common tasks such as saving and opening a file, printing, and checking spelling.

style   A preformatted arrangement of groups within an organization chart.

table   Information that you organize in columns and rows so you can present it in a way that is easy to read and understand. You must have Microsoft Word for Windows installed on your computer to create tables in PowerPoint.

Table AutoFormat   A feature that adds predesigned formatting to tables. Each Table AutoFormat includes borders, colors, patterns, and formatting.

text block   A box in which you enter and edit text. Each "Click to add text" placeholder is a text block.

three-dimensional   *See* 3-D.

thumbnail   A miniature view of a slide or design template. A thumbnail gives you an idea of what your slide looks like, but it is probably too small to actually read.

transition   An effect that determines how one slide advances to the next during a slide show. You can apply a different transition to each slide in your presentation.

Undo   A command that enables you to reverse a previous action. The Standard toolbar contains an Undo button.

views   Ways in which PowerPoint enables you to examine the information in your presentation. PowerPoint views include Outline, Slide, Slide Sorter, Notes Pages, and Slide Show. You switch between views using the buttons to the left of the horizontal scroll bar (in the lower-left corner of the screen).

WordArt   A feature that transforms text into interesting shapes. With WordArt, you can use different fonts, colors, and shadows to create text for a corporate logo. You must install Microsoft WordArt on your computer to use WordArt.

Write-Up   Feature that enables you to choose how to print handouts for yourself or your audience.

X-axis   The horizontal reference line in a chart.

Y-axis   The vertical reference line in a chart.

Z-axis   In a 3-D chart, the z-axis represents the reference line that gives the chart its depth; the reference line goes from front to back.

Index

Symbols

3-D
    charts, 136, 150
    defined, 237

A

Action Items, 178
    defined, 187, 237
    designing with Meeting Minder, 187-188
    printing, 188-190
active
    files, 33
    slides, 21
AGaramond font, 43
alignment (justification)
    defined, 239
    text
        charts, 145
        moving aligned text, 63
        slides, 43, 62-63
Alignment command (Format menu), 63, 231
animation effects (special effects) 194, 201-203, 237
    Camera Effect, 201
Animation Effects toolbar, 203
Animation Settings dialog box, 199
Answer Wizard, Help Topics, 35
Apply Design Template dialog box, 19
arrow pointer, four-headed, 167
artwork, *see* clip art; WordArt
ascending order (table data), 126
assistants position (organization charts), 94
    undoing deletions, 102
attributes, defined, 237
    see also formatting
AutoContent Wizard, 9
    designing presentations, 13-15
        title slide, 14
    viewing, 12

AutoContent Wizard dialog box, 14-15
AutoCorrect, 55-56
    deleting entries in list, 56
    storing "shorthand" for terms, 56
AutoCorrect (automatic spell checking), 42
AutoCorrect command (Tools menu), 56
AutoFormat (automatic formatting)
    tables, 113, 131-132
        Table AutoFormat, 242
AutoLayouts, 9, 42, 237
    bulleted lists, 237
    slides, 20-23
AutoShapes, *see* also clip art; WordArt
axes (charts), 136, 242

B

balloon comments 88-89
bar charts, 136
bold formatting
    text, 57-58
    toolbar buttons, toggling, 58
borders, tables, 128-130
Borders and Shading command (Format menu), 129
Build Slide Text command (Tools menu), 199
building slide text, 237
Bullet command (Format menu), 65
Bullet dialog box, 65
bulleted lists
    bullets
        changing, 64-65
        defined, 237
    defined, 237
    designing, 221
        inserting in slides, 23
buttons, toolbars
    Outline toolbar, 165
    toggling formatting buttons, 58
    ToolTips (names of buttons), 8

C

Camera Effect (special effects), 201
cancelling spell checking, 54
Cell Height and Width dialog box, 121
cells
    defined, 237
    charts, undoing mistakes, 140
    tables, 115
center-aligning text, 63
charts
    3-D, 136, 150, 237
    axes, 136, 242
    bar charts, 136
    cells, undoing mistakes, 140
    column charts, 136
    data, defined, 238
    data points, defined, 136
    data series, defined, 136
    data-entry, 141-142
    defined, 238
    designing, 227
    formatting text, 143-144
        alignment, 145
    inserting on slides, 138-140
    legends, defined, 239
    opening, 142
    Organization Chart program, installing, 95
    pie charts, 136
    resizing, 148
    titles, inserting, 146-148
    types, changing, 149-151
    see also organization charts
check boxes, 238
Clear command (Edit menu), 47
"click to add text" placeholder, 238
clicking mouse, double-clicking, 238
clip art, 68
    ClipArt Gallery, 68
        finding clip art, 68, 71
        editing category list, 85
        inserting pictures, 84-87
        updating list, 85
    color (recoloring), 82-83